RAND JUSTICE, INFRASTRUCTURE, AND ENVIRONMENT

T0108557

How Can Workers' Compensation Systems Promote Occupational Safety and Health?

Stakeholder Views on Policy and Research Priorities

Michael Dworsky, Nicholas Broten

For more information on this publication, visit www.rand.org/t/RR2566

Library of Congress Cataloging-in-Publication Data is available for this publication.
ISBN: 978-1-9774-0151-9

Support RAND
Make a tax-deductible charitable contribution at
www.rand.org/giving/contribute

www.rand.org

Preface

Workers' compensation is a state-level social insurance program that provides financial, medical, and rehabilitation benefits to workers who sustain job-related injuries or illnesses. Workers, employers, and other stakeholders involved in workers' compensation systems have long voiced concerns about the extent to which workers' compensation promotes occupational safety and health (OSH) and the well-being of injured workers; government reports and journalistic accounts in recent years have both highlighted perennial issues and documented emerging concerns. Key topic areas highlighted in these accounts include *prevention of injury and disability*; *system coverage, benefit adequacy, and cost spillovers*; *claim management processes*; and *occupational health care*. Despite the awareness of these issues across stakeholder groups, it is not clear how much consensus there is about which of these challenges to OSH in the workers' compensation system are most pressing, whether there is sufficient evidence to identify best practices, or what structural barriers have prevented policymakers from resolving these challenges.

The National Institute for Occupational Safety and Health (NIOSH) requested that RAND explore the beliefs and priorities of key workers' compensation stakeholder groups about system challenges and research priorities that, if addressed, would be most useful for reforming workers' compensation systems to promote OSH and the well-being of workers. RAND conducted a literature scan to identify published criticisms of current workers' compensation systems, focusing on the implications of workers' compensation for worker safety, health, and economic well-being. After producing a compendium of such perspectives, RAND then convened a series of stakeholder conversations with selected representatives from five stakeholder groups. This report describes stakeholder views and attempts to synthesize these perspectives to offer suggestions for research and policy-analysis priorities likely to make workers' compensation policy more effective at promoting the health and well-being of workers.

The research reported here was conducted in the RAND Justice Policy Program, which spans both criminal and civil justice system issues with such topics as public safety, effective policing, police–community relations, drug policy and enforcement, corrections policy, use of technology in law enforcement, tort reform, catastrophe and mass-injury compensation, court resourcing, and insurance regulation. Program research is supported by government agencies, foundations, and the private sector.

RAND Justice, Infrastructure, and Environment (JIE) conducts research and analysis in civil and criminal justice, infrastructure development and financing, environmental policy, transportation planning and technology, immigration and border protection, public and occupational safety, energy policy, science and innovation policy, space, telecommunications, and trends and implications of artificial intelligence and other computational technologies.

Questions or comments about this report should be sent to the project leader, Michael Dworsky (mdworsky@rand.org). For more information about RAND Justice Policy, see www.rand.org/jie/justice-policy or contact the director at justice@rand.org.

Contents

Preface iii

Tables vii

Summary viii

    Findings ix

        Published Critiques Identified Numerous Problems with Current Workers'
            Compensation Policy ix

        Stakeholders Identified Many Shortcomings of Workers' Compensation Policy as
            Important Challenges to Worker Outcomes x

        Policy Priorities and Research Needs Suggest a Two-Pronged Research Agenda for
            Improving Workers' Compensation Policy xii

Acknowledgments xiv

Abbreviations xv

Chapter One. Introduction 1

Chapter Two. Objectives and Recent Critiques of Workers' Compensation Policy 3

    Goals of Workers' Compensation Systems 3

        Early Development and the Grand Bargain 3

        The National Commission on State Workmen's Compensation Laws 4

        Recent Published Perspectives 5

        Workers' Compensation Today 8

Chapter Three. Stakeholder Views of System Challenges 10

    Overview of Challenges Identified as Major Priorities 11

    Limitations 12

    Prevention of Injury and Disability 13

        Incentives Based on Workers' Compensation Costs or Injury Rates Have
            Unintended Consequences 13

        Safety Interventions Were Viewed as More Promising Than Incentive Programs and
            Less Likely to Create Incentives for Underreporting 14

        Inadequate Investment in Disability Prevention After Injury 15

    System Coverage, Benefit Adequacy, and Cost Spillovers 15

        Coverage of Alternative Work Arrangements 15

        Coverage of Conditions: Work-Relatedness and Causation 16

        Inadequate Benefits and Cost Spillovers to Other Social and Health Insurance Programs .. 17

    Claim Management Processes 18

        Too Litigious and Difficult to Navigate for Workers, Small Employers 18

        Focus on Compliance Leads to Complexity and Distracts from Other Objectives 19

Data Management and Claim Tracking Problems Within Employers.................................. 19

Occupational Health Care... 19

    Lack of Integration with Other Health Care 20

    Poor-Quality Care 21

Payment Reform and Quality Improvement... 22

Political Economy and Workers' Compensation Reform... 23

Chapter Four. Policy Options and Research Needs 24

Policy Priorities... 25

    Removing Barriers to Claiming and System Navigation... 25

    Injury and Disability Prevention Programs... 26

    Priorities for Occupational Health Care Delivery... 30

Evidence Needed to Improve Outcomes and Policymaking 34

    Causation of Occupational Diseases and Nontraumatic Injuries............................. 34

    Improving Dispute Resolution 35

    Evidence on Cost Spillovers from Workers' Compensation to Other Insurance Systems ... 37

    Technological Change, Work Arrangements, and Evolving Labor Laws 37

Chapter Five. Suggestions for a Research Agenda to Improve Workers' Compensation Policy. 39

Priorities for the National Institute for Occupational Safety and Health and Other

    Federal Research on Workers' Compensation.. 42

Appendix A: Discussion Participants 47

Appendix B: Overview of Workers' Compensation Systems 48

Overview of Workers' Compensation Systems.. 48

    Types of Benefits 49

    Financing and Delivery... 53

    Federal Programs 54

Appendix C: Compendium of Critical Perspectives on Current Workers' Compensation

    Policy 56

Background... 56

Goals of Contemporary Workers' Compensation Systems 57

Overview of Key Workers' Compensation Policy Issues 58

    Workers' Compensation Strengths 58

    Workers' Compensation Challenges.. 59

Addendum: Supporting Quotations 68

    Workers' Compensation Strengths 68

    Workers' Compensation Challenges.. 71

References... 90

Tables

Table 3.1: Overview of Workers' Compensation Policy Challenges Identified by
      Stakeholder Groups.. 11
Table 4.1: Policy Options and Research Needs Identified by Stakeholder Groups...................... 25
Table 5.1: Potential Research Funders and Research Priorities 40
Table A.1: Stakeholder Group Discussion Participants.. 47

Summary

Workers' compensation is a state-level social insurance program that provides financial, medical, and rehabilitation benefits to workers who sustain occupational injuries or illnesses. Workers, employers, and other stakeholders involved in workers' compensation systems have long voiced concerns about the extent to which workers' compensation serves to promote occupational safety and health (OSH) and the well-being of injured workers, while government reports and journalistic accounts in recent years have both highlighted perennial issues and documented emerging concerns. However, it is not clear how much consensus there is about which of the challenges to OSH and worker well-being in the workers' compensation system are most pressing, whether there is sufficient evidence to identify best practices or policy solutions, or what structural barriers have prevented policymakers from resolving these challenges.

The National Institute for Occupational Safety and Health (NIOSH) requested that RAND explore the beliefs and priorities of key workers' compensation stakeholder groups about system challenges and research priorities that, if addressed, would be most useful for reforming workers' compensation systems to promote OSH and the well-being of workers. This report describes stakeholder views on the most pressing challenges and priorities for workers' compensation systems and attempts to synthesize these perspectives to offer suggestions for research and policy analysis priorities. To address these questions, RAND conducted a literature scan to identify published criticisms of current workers' compensation systems, focusing on the implications of workers' compensation for workers' safety, health, and economic well-being. After producing a compendium of such critical perspectives, RAND then convened a series of stakeholder conversations with selected representatives from five key stakeholder groups:

- workers
- employers
- claims administrators
- state agency leaders
- occupational health care providers.

Workers and employers are the core stakeholders of a workers' compensation system, and every system must strike an acceptable balance between the interests of workers and employers to remain politically sustainable. The other three stakeholder groups invited to participate in this study were chosen because they are crucially important in setting workers' compensation policy (state agencies), in managing the operations of the workers' compensation system and shaping the practical realities experienced by injured workers (claims administrators), or in providing needed medical care and helping manage the recovery and return-to-work processes (health care providers).

Certain limitations to the scope and findings of this study are important to bear in mind. We had relatively small numbers of stakeholder participants, and while we sought to achieve a diversity of backgrounds and experience within each stakeholder group, we did not attempt to select a representative sample of stakeholders. Other system participants (such as attorneys or vocational rehabilitation professionals) that were not included in these conversations may also have constructive viewpoints on system challenges.

Findings

The findings of this study can be organized into three groupings. First, we have distilled major themes from published critiques of workers' compensation policy (Chapter Two). Second, we gathered stakeholder perspectives on the most important system challenges (Chapter Three). Third, we identified policy solutions and research needs suggested by stakeholders (Chapter Four). In general, stakeholders agreed with the published critiques but placed a greater emphasis on concerns about health care delivery, return to work, and injury prevention than, in our view, some of the published critiques had.

Stakeholders identified promising policy interventions in need of rigorous evaluation and also suggested research on questions of epidemiology and system organization that could help to guide state workers' compensation policymaking in directions more likely to promote OSH than current practice.

Published Critiques Identified Numerous Problems with Current Workers' Compensation Policy

RAND's review of published perspectives on workers' compensation policy identified several major themes:

- **Coverage remains less than universal, and benefit adequacy is insufficient**. Many state policy changes have had the effect of making it more difficult for workers to access benefits and needed care, while the rise of alternative work arrangements has left a growing class of workers outside the workers' compensation system altogether. Meanwhile, disability benefits are often inadequate to protect workers from the earnings losses they actually experience after injury or illness. When workers are inadequately compensated for their injuries within the workers' compensation system, earnings losses and medical costs may be borne by workers and their families or may be borne by health insurers or public social insurance programs in the form of cost spillovers.
- **Significant problems remain in disability determination and medical treatment**. States differ widely in their approaches to determining permanent disability; widely used approaches are not evidence-based and may be conceptually inappropriate. In addition, medical care provided to injured workers is often of low quality despite increasing levels of spending, leading to avoidable disability and loss of function (at best) or severe iatrogenic harms, such as opioid addiction and death (at worst).

- **Challenges remain in vocational rehabilitation and return to work**. Return-to-work outcomes for many types of workers and at many employers remain poor, exacerbating the economic impact of injury on workers and their families.
- **Safety promotion practices have been somewhat successful but create complex claiming incentives**. Existing injury surveillance systems and incentives for safety provided by employers or by workers' compensation premium setting can lead to perverse incentives for the suppression of injury reporting.
- **System complexity is a drag on performance**. Complexity, delays, and excessive disputes within workers' compensation systems have been widely criticized as a factor that raises system costs and that can harm injured workers by creating an adversarial relationship with employers or preventing timely receipt of needed medical care and rehabilitation services.

Further background on workers' compensation system objectives and historical development is presented in Chapter Two, along with an elaboration of the above themes. The compendium of critical perspectives that resulted from our literature review is included as Appendix C to this report.

Stakeholders Identified Many Shortcomings of Workers' Compensation Policy as Important Challenges to Worker Outcomes

In general, stakeholders affirmed the accuracy of many published criticisms of workers' compensation policy. While the areas of greatest emphasis varied slightly across stakeholders, there were many system problems that were identified as serious problems demanding more research attention and policy innovation.

New Approaches to Injury Prevention and Disability Management Are Needed

Although workers' compensation provides financial incentives for safety through experience-rating of premiums, workers and health care providers felt that financial incentives had important limitations. More active safety interventions provided by state workers' compensation agencies or by some workers' compensation insurers were viewed as more promising approaches to injury prevention, particularly for small employers. Similarly, a greater emphasis on prevention or management of work disability following injury was identified as an important priority that relatively few state systems have pursued in major ways.

Declining Coverage of Workers and Health Conditions Prevents Workers' Compensation from Serving Its Purposes

Workers' compensation has traditionally provided near-universal coverage, but stakeholders voiced serious concern about erosion of that coverage along two dimensions. Alternative work arrangements—such as temporary-agency workers or independent contractors—have been growing as a share of the workforce, and stakeholders felt that these workers often failed to access the workers' compensation system (when they were covered) or found themselves shut out entirely due to their lack of employee status. Meanwhile, higher standards for causation and attempts to limit employer exposure to preexisting conditions or nonwork disability were also viewed as a harmful erosion of coverage by some stakeholders. Interestingly, employers and claims administrators (who have strong interests in controlling system costs) also felt that current approaches to causation, apportionment, preexisting conditions, and coverage of occupational diseases had major shortcomings and led to excessive disputes.

Inefficient Claim Management and Dispute Resolution Processes Harm Workers and Drive Up Costs

Some stakeholders identified deficiencies in claims management processes, particularly excessive litigation and other inefficient forms of dispute resolution. Stakeholders also expressed a view that oversight and administration of workers' compensation systems often focused on compliance with bureaucratic requirements that bore little relation to worker outcomes, in part because compliance is simple to monitor while worker outcomes reflect many factors and may be difficult to monitor. Meanwhile, workers are often unable to navigate current systems without attorney representation, while system complexity can also deter workers from filing claims in the first place. Stakeholders felt that current approaches to dispute resolution, the adversarial nature of the system, and a narrow focus on compliance impeded communication between workers, employers, and health care providers and often prevented stakeholders from focusing on worker outcomes.

Health Care for Injured Workers Is Often Fragmented and of Low Quality and Is Not Designed to Reward Worker Outcomes

By far the most widely shared concern about current workers' compensation systems was the view that health care delivery in workers' compensation was not coordinated with the rest of the health care system and that the provision of poor-quality care in isolation from the rest of health care severely harmed workers. The overprescribing of opioids by workers' compensation providers is an example that has received widespread attention, but the overuse of spinal surgery and other frequently high-risk and low-value care is also a major concern. Disputes over compensability or lack of provider access within workers' compensation, meanwhile, were identified as barriers to the timely provision of needed care. The lack of integration between workers' compensation and other health care payers and between occupational medicine providers and other physicians who might be involved in a patient's care were raised by diverse stakeholder groups. Similarly, stakeholders felt that the broader health care system often failed to examine, let alone promote, workers' functional status. The management of chronic conditions that are highly prevalent in workers' compensation populations (such as musculoskeletal disorders) was an area where greater integration between occupational medicine and the broader health care system was sorely needed.

Policy Priorities and Research Needs Suggest a Two-Pronged Research Agenda for Improving Workers' Compensation Policy

Research needed to inform an optimal system and best practices might proceed along two tracks. First, state policy experimentation in workers' compensation could be encouraged in part by federal investments and support for rigorous, independent evaluations. Stakeholders also identified a need for a wide range of more basic scientific, economic, and other social-scientific evidence on questions like epidemiology, system performance, and financing. Many important questions, particularly those related to causation, apportionment, and occupational disease presumptions, will generally require observational study and epidemiological methods rather than program evaluation. The missions of NIOSH and other federal research funders are compatible with research along both these tracks.

Stakeholders Attached a High Priority to Development of New Models and Interventions for Health Care Delivery, Injury Prevention, Dispute Resolution, and Disability Prevention

Stakeholders identified examples of promising state-level innovations for injury prevention, return to work and disability prevention after injury, quality improvement in occupational health care, and integration of functional outcomes into health care. Relatively few of these interventions have been subjected to rigorous, independent evaluation, while the generalizability of those that have shown favorable evaluation results to states and sectors with very different health systems, workers' compensation markets, or labor relations is not well understood. Stakeholders felt that the severe problems with workers' compensation health care called out for innovative solutions and state experimentation, with respect to both improving the existing delivery system and improving integration with the broader health care system.

Scientific Evidence on Causation Is Badly Needed to Guide Workers' Compensation Systems in Handling Occupational Disease and Preexisting Conditions

Several stakeholder groups expressed hope that the development of better data sets for monitoring worker health could lead to a better understanding of causation and work-relatedness for occupational diseases and nontraumatic injuries. One area where best practices were felt to be missing was in the apportionment of disability to nonoccupational cause and the development of presumptions optimized to reflect scientific evidence and minimize dispute costs. A more definitive and current list of occupational diseases that should be presumptively covered would be a valuable policy contribution, but such a list would require a far-reaching epidemiological effort and, likely, the development of new longitudinal data sets linking health status, work histories, and nonoccupational exposures for large populations. Similarly, questions about the consequences of injury, factors influencing return-to-work outcomes, and the extent of cost spillovers onto other social programs could be addressed more effectively with the more extensive use of longitudinal data sets combining workers' compensation claims with other administrative records. NIOSH and other federal research funders might play a role in enabling the development of such large-scale data sets, while funders focused on specific health problems might support more detailed investigation of how occupational and nonoccupational risk factors affect worker health.

The National Institute for Occupational Safety and Health Should Play a Larger Role in the Evaluation and Dissemination of Workers' Compensation Policies and Best Practices Related to Occupational Safety and Health

In addition to the evaluation of specific policy interventions, stakeholders felt that workers' compensation policymakers often lacked knowledge about best practices for relatively narrow but consequential aspects of system administration, such as rules governing claim initiation, attorney fees, and so on, with the relevant expertise often concentrated in interested parties (for example, the insurance industry). Meanwhile, state policymakers might have difficulty recognizing such best practices or considering the full range of policy variation across all the state workers' compensation systems.

Stakeholders lamented that a model or ideal workers' compensation system had not been identified. Although stakeholder groups other than workers were skeptical of an explicit federal role in workers' compensation policymaking or financing, all stakeholder groups felt that federal research organizations have an important role to play in analyzing and disseminating best practices with respect to system design and administration. Mixed-methods research approaches in the spirit of health services research might help to provide rigor to efforts to identify and disseminate best practices. Questions related to the coordination of workers' compensation with other health care payers and public social insurance programs, meanwhile, will likely require observational studies or the adoption of theoretical and statistical frameworks that allow explicit analysis of quantities like cost spillovers from workplace injury or the identification of optimal financing mechanisms for intervention programs or quality improvement efforts.

Although stakeholders identified a large array of system challenges, there was no shortage of promising initiatives awaiting evaluation, best practices waiting to be identified, or scientific and social-scientific questions in need of answers to guide policy formation. The stakeholder perspectives collected and synthesized in this report may aid in the selection of priorities by NIOSH and other research funders interested in promoting OSH and worker well-being.

Acknowledgments

We wish to thank a number of people and entities for their contributions to this study. Thanks are due to several RAND staff and researchers, including Jayne Gordon for assistance with invitations and scheduling, Nupur Nanda for research assistance, and Chris Nelson for advising on study design. The Compendium of Critical Perspectives included as Appendix C of this report benefited from input provided by an informal group of subject matter experts, including Les Boden of the Boston University School of Public Health, H. Allan Hunt of the W. E. Upjohn Institute, Jeff Eddinger of the National Council on Compensation Insurance, Jennifer Wolf-Horejsh of the International Association of Industrial Accident Boards and Commissions (IAIABC), Marjorie Baldwin of Arizona State University, Emily Spieler of the Northeastern University School of Law, and John F. Burton, Jr. of Rutgers University. IAIABC staff provided invaluable inputs at several stages of this research. We also wish to thank Philip Armour at RAND and Gregory Warner at the Harvard T. H. Chan School of Public Health for their insightful and remarkably thorough work as this study's quality assurance reviewers. We also with to thank NIOSH staff, including Steve Wurzelbacher, Tim Bushnell, and Rene Pana-Cryan, for helping to frame the study and providing input throughout the research process; finally, we wish to thank Dr. John Howard for initiating the discussions that ultimately led to preparation of this report.

Abbreviations

BLS	Bureau of Labor Statistics
BWC	Bureau of Workers' Compensation
CMS	Centers for Medicaid and Medicare Services
COHE	Center for Occupational Health Excellence
COR	certificate of recognition
DCBS	Department of Consumer and Business Services
DOL	Department of Labor
DOL ODEP	Department of Labor Office of Disability Employment Policy
DOWC	Division of Workers' Compensation
DSH	Division of Safety and Hygiene
EAIP	Employer-at-Injury Program
FMLA	Family Medical Leave Act
IAIABC	International Association of Industrial Accident Boards and Commissions
L&I	Labor and Industries
MCC	major contributory cause
NASI	National Academy of Social Insurance
NIOSH	National Institute for Occupational Safety and Health
NYS OHCN	New York State Occupational Health Clinic Network
OSH	occupational safety and health
OSHA	Occupational Safety and Health Administration
PPD	permanent partial disability
PWP	Preferred Worker Program
QPOP	Quality Performance and Outcomes Payments
SIG	Safety Intervention Grant
SSA	Social Security Agency
SSDI	Social Security Disability Insurance
TTD	temporary total disability
WC	workers' compensation
WCD	Workers' Compensation Division

Chapter One. Introduction

Workers' compensation provides disability benefits and needed medical care to workers who suffer occupational injury or illness (injured workers), and a widely recognized objective of workers' compensation systems is to encourage the provision of safe workplaces and provide for the effective rehabilitation of injured workers (National Commission on State Workmen's Compensation Laws, 1972). The design and performance of workers' compensation systems therefore have substantial implications for occupational safety and health (OSH) and the postinjury outcomes of injured workers, key concerns for the National Institute for Occupational Safety and Health (NIOSH).[1]

Given the presence of intrinsic conflicts between the interests of different stakeholder groups (particularly workers and employers), workers' compensation policymaking is frequently contentious, and workers' compensation systems face many policy challenges. Many of these challenges are longstanding—concerns about the adequacy of benefits within the system, for example, echo similar concerns from the 1970s, while discussions about efforts to allow employers to forego workers' compensation coverage mirror debates from the origins of the system in the early twentieth century. Nonetheless, several recent governmental and journalistic accounts have focused attention on current points of disagreement and tension in the system today. A common thread in some of these perspectives, which are discussed in more detail in Chapter Two, is the notion that the balance of power between worker and employer interests in setting workers' compensation policy has, in recent years, shifted toward employers to the detriment of workers.

NIOSH requested that RAND explore the beliefs of key workers' compensation stakeholder groups about system challenges and research priorities. In this report, RAND sought to gather and synthesize stakeholder perspectives about which policy options and research efforts are most important for reforming workers' compensation policy to promote OSH and the well-being of workers. As part of this effort, RAND sought to identify conflicts or tensions among advocated policy goals, including areas where specific system features, policy choices, or practices have unintended consequences for workers. The findings of this study are intended to help NIOSH

---

[1] OSH is a broad concept that covers mental and physical hazards within the workplace and other factors that affect worker health. Besides posing a threat to worker health, occupational injury and illness can lead to poor outcomes for workers and their families, including loss of employment, economic hardship, and reduced quality of life. In this report, we use the term "well-being" to refer broadly to economic and noneconomic outcomes other than health status for injured workers, particularly employment, family income, and functional status or nonwork disability. Worker well-being is sometimes defined more broadly as an integrative concept representing the relationship between physical and environmental factors, worker health, job characteristics and policies, and social and community factors on an individual's quality of life and ability to thrive in the workplace (Chari et al., 2018).

and other organizations that already focus on OSH or workers' compensation policy to identify research priorities, as well as to inform other policymakers, stakeholders, and funders about topics in workers' compensation policy that are relevant to their missions.

To develop such a prioritization of challenges and research directions in workers' compensation, RAND conducted a literature scan to identify published criticisms of current workers' compensation systems, focusing on the implications of workers' compensation for worker safety, health, and economic well-being. After producing a compendium of such critical perspectives (included as Appendix C to this report), RAND then convened a series of stakeholder conversations with selected representatives from five stakeholder groups:

- workers
- employers
- claims administrators
- state agency leaders
- occupational health care providers.

RAND convened separate conference calls with each of these groups between February and April 2018. This report provides a synthesis of these discussions and identifies priorities for policy evaluation and other research. Chapter Two provides background on the objectives of workers' compensation policy and briefly summarizes major themes from the literature scan. Chapter Three reviews stakeholder discussion about the major policy challenges in workers' compensation today. Chapter Four identifies promising policy initiatives and areas where better evidence or additional research is anticipated by stakeholders to have the greatest impact on worker outcomes. Chapter Five concludes the report, sketching a framework for future research efforts aimed at improving occupational health and safety through better workers' compensation policy.

Chapter Two. Objectives and Recent Critiques of Workers' Compensation Policy

This chapter presents a brief overview of recent policy developments in workers' compensation and summarizes policy challenges RAND identified in a scan of published perspectives on workers' compensation systems. Readers without extensive domain knowledge of workers' compensation are encouraged to consult Appendix B, which provides an overview. A more complete list of policy issues and supporting quotations from the literature can be found in Appendix C.

Goals of Workers' Compensation Systems

Early Development and the Grand Bargain

Before workers' compensation systems were established in the early twentieth century, the only channel through which an employee could receive payment from their employer for damages related to a workplace injury was a negligence lawsuit (Burton, 2017). This arrangement created problems for employers and employees. Under the negligence liability system, employers were required to demonstrate "due care" in protecting employees from occupational risks (Fishback and Kantor, 2007). To successfully win damages, injured workers had to prove this standard had not been met. Employers used several common-law defenses to avoid liability. One approach, known as the *fellow-servant rule*, was to demonstrate that a coworker of the injured worker, and not the employer, was responsible for the injury. Another defense was *assumption of risk*, or the claim that the employee was aware of the risks of the job when accepting the employment contract. The third defense in the so-called unholy trinity was *contributory negligence*, in which any negligence on the part of the worker prevented recovery. These and other legal defenses meant that many injured employees who filed negligence claims against their employer and had to incur potentially large legal fees received no compensation. The negligence system also created cost uncertainty for employers, particularly because damages sought in a lawsuit could include noneconomic costs related to pain, suffering, and wrongful death.

The establishment of workers' compensation systems represented a compromise, or "grand bargain," that provided partial solutions to the problems employers and employees faced under the negligence liability system. From the employee perspective, no-fault benefits dramatically reduced the burden of proof for receiving compensation, from proving an injury is the result of employer negligence to showing it is work related. The grand bargain arrangement was also meant to reduce the time between injury and necessary medical treatment by eliminating potentially lengthy court proceedings through no-fault coverage. From the employer perspective, the grand bargain created greater certainty about costs and gave employers immunity from noneconomic damages. Employees raised their expected compensation from workplace injuries, mostly driven by a larger share of injuries receiving some compensation, but gave up access to full damages. Employers, meanwhile, eliminated the risk of potentially very costly litigation by agreeing instead to pay workers' compensation premiums on a regular basis (Fishback and Kantor, 2007).

The National Commission on State Workmen's Compensation Laws

In contrast to the major social insurance systems that emerged as part of the New Deal or afterward, workers' compensation is entirely the prerogative of the states and has never been subject to any federal standards. Nor has the federal government played a significant role in identifying or disseminating best practices across states.

However, a landmark national effort to assess the state of workers' compensation policies and establish consensus about effective workers' compensation practices was the 1972 National Commission on State Workmen's Compensation Laws, an effort created by the Occupational Safety and Health (OSH) Act of 1970. The mandate of the national commission was to "undertake a comprehensive study and evaluation of State workmen's compensation laws in order to determine if such laws provide an adequate, prompt, and equitable system of compensation" (National Commission on State Workmen's Compensation Laws, 1972).

The national commission identified five key objectives of workers' compensation policies:

1. broad coverage of employees and work-related injuries and diseases
2. substantial protection against interruption of income
3. provision of sufficient medical care and rehabilitation services
4. encouragement of safety
5. an effective system for delivery of benefits and services.

State workers' compensation policies were found to be lacking in many of these dimensions. At the time of the report, approximately 85 percent of employees were covered by workers' compensation insurance, which the commission deemed "inadequate." Gaps in coverage were driven primarily by variation in state rules regarding which classes of workers could be left out of the workers' compensation system and the tradition of voluntary coverage in many states. The commission highlighted coverage gaps for low-wage workers, such as employees of agricultural employees and small firms, as particularly problematic and recommended making workers' compensation insurance compulsory for all employers and extending coverage to most classes of employees who were at the time excluded. Other recommendations included full coverage for all work-related diseases and developing a master list of compensable occupational illnesses.

The commission also found cash benefits in the workers' compensation system to be generally inadequate. For example, the maximum weekly benefit in more than half of the states was less than the national poverty threshold for a family of four. The commission also highlighted inequities in cash benefits: benefit levels varied considerable across states, and statutory benefit maximums meant that low-wage workers tended to fare better than high-wage workers on a relative basis. In fact, because weekly benefits were capped at a percentage of average state wages, roughly half of indemnity beneficiaries received less than two-thirds of their lost pay. The commission recommended implementing progressive increases in maximum benefit levels and ensuring payments were at least 80 percent of spendable, or after-tax, earnings.

The national commission characterized the provision of medical care in the workers' compensation system as "reasonably good" and the provision of vocational rehabilitation services as "less successful." The commission recommended injured workers have initial choice of physician for workers' compensation–related medical care, either selected from all medical providers in their state or a list of approved occupational doctors. Further, the commission recommended there be no statutory restrictions on the duration of medical treatment or the expense of medical and vocational rehabilitation treatments related to workplace injuries. Regarding the administration of these services, the commission suggested each state establish its own medical rehabilitation division with supervising authority and a special mandate to ensure all eligible injured workers receive treatment.

Regarding the promotion of safety in the workers' compensation system, the national commission endorsed extending experience modification programs to as many employers as possible and recommended workers' compensation insurers provide loss prevention services to covered employers.

Finally, the national commission identified six core responsibilities of state workers' compensation agencies and provided suggestions for improvement. These responsibilities are (1) administering the state workers' compensation statute, (2) providing continuing review of the statute and recommending changes to it and related policies, (3) informing employees of their rights and responsibilities under the law, (4) informing employers and carriers of their rights and responsibilities under the law, (5) assisting with dispute resolution, and (6) adjudicating disputes, if needed. Notable administrative recommendations of the commission included regulating attorney fees and establishing the time limit for filing a claim at three years after the claimant became aware of an injury.

Recent Published Perspectives

Since 1972, workers' compensation stakeholders have assessed the extent to which the national commission's recommendations have been implemented across states, as well as the overall health and sustainability of workers' compensation systems. RAND conducted an informal review of critical perspectives on workers' compensation policy published over the past decade. This review started with studies and viewpoints the authors were familiar with and suggestions from NIOSH. An initial draft was circulated to a group of over a dozen researchers and subject matter experts to identify writings and topics that had been neglected, which were then incorporated into the review. This review document is included as Appendix C to this report.

The following are the major system criticisms identified in our review of recently published perspectives:

Prevention of Injury and Disability

- **Safety promotion practices have been somewhat successful, but create complex claiming incentives**. While injury rates in general have declined, observers pointed out that many preventable workplace injuries still occur each year, and injury rates are more highly concentrated among temporary, leased, contingent,[1] and informal workers (OSHA, 2015; Silverstein, 2010). Some observed that safety incentive programs, such as experience-rating or behavior-based incentives, may discourage legitimate claiming by changing workplace attitudes toward employees who file a claim (Morantz et al., 2016). Others suggested the provision of no-cost medical treatment for work-related injuries may motivate workers to overstate the extent to which their injury is work related (Lynch, 2017).
- **Challenges remain in vocational rehabilitation and return to work**. Return-to-work outcomes are unequal across the wage distribution, and some evidence suggests more vulnerable workers return to employment sooner, possibly due to a liquidity effect (Galizzi et al., 2016; Boden and Galizzi, 2016). Observers have noted some workers are incentivized to return to work too early, while employers sometimes underinvest in efforts to return their employees to the workplace because the costs of absences are distributed across many stakeholders (Belton, 2010; IAIABC Disability Management and Return to Work Committee, 2016; Savych and Thumula, 2017).

System Coverage, Benefit Adequacy, and Cost Spillovers

- **Coverage remains less than universal**. Observers noted that many of the coverage restrictions identified in the national commission report are still in place, such as exclusions for small employers and agricultural workers (DOL, 2016). Also, full-time employees are sometimes misclassified as independent contractors and are, therefore,

---

[1] The Bureau of Labor Statistics (BLS) distinguishes between two broad groups of workers in nontraditional work arrangements:

- "**Contingent workers** are people who do not expect their jobs to last or who report that their jobs are temporary. They do not have an implicit or explicit contract for ongoing employment.
- "**Alternative employment arrangements** include independent contractors, on-call workers, temporary help agency workers, and workers provided by contract firms."

BLS notes that "a person's job may be defined as both contingent and an alternative employment arrangement, but this is not automatically the case because contingency is defined separately from the four alternative work arrangements." We use the term "alternative work arrangements" to orient discussion in this report, although "contingent workers" is often used to refer broadly to workers in either type of nontraditional work arrangement. We note that temporary agency employees, who are covered by the workers' compensation system and are the subject of a growing amount of research, fall into both categories (BLS, 2018).

excluded from coverage (Carre, 2015). The rise of alternative work arrangements and the contingent workforce have led to concerns about insufficient coverage for those workers (Duff, 2018; Spieler, 2017; Silverstein, 2010). Exclusions of specific injuries and diseases and efforts to apportion the work-relatedness of injuries and diseases, particularly those involving preexisting conditions, also tend to reduce overall coverage (DOL, 2016).

- **Benefit adequacy is insufficient**. Statutory limits on benefits and compensability have had the effect of reducing the adequacy of and access to benefits for many workers below the standard set by the national commission (Burton, 2017; DOL, 2016; Spieler, 2017). Since 2002, an estimated 33 states have reduced benefits or made it more difficult to qualify for benefits (Grabell and Berkes, 2015b).

- **Societal costs of work-related injuries are not fully covered by workers' compensation**. Cost spillovers from workers' compensation to other social insurance programs, such as Social Security Disability Insurance (SSDI) and Medicare, place additional strain on those programs and reduce incentives for worker safety (OSHA, 2015; Leigh and Marcin, 2012; DOL, 2016; Morantz et al., 2016). Costs of occupational injuries extend beyond social insurance programs, to workers' families and communities (Asfaw et al., 2015; Strunin and Boden, 2004a).

Claim Management Processes

- **System complexity is a drag on performance**. Several observers noted that the administration of workers' compensation is often too complex, which can lead to confusion, uncertainty, a slow claims process, a focus on compliance rather than outcomes, and disparities in outcomes across categories of workers and across states (North, 2010; Groeger, Grabell, and Cotts, 2015). Also, some have pointed out that the ability of state agencies to oversee and regulate workers' compensation programs is limited by resource constraints (Crum, 2010).

- **Dispute resolution is too complex and slow**. Lengthy disputes, often driven by uncertainties in injury causation, can delay cash benefits and essential medical services (DOL, 2016).

- **Compromise and release settlements are controversial**. The prevalence of settlements has increased in the last four decades, in part due to backlogs in disputes (Hunt and Barth, 2010). Vulnerable workers may feel pressured to enter into settlement agreements with employers and insurers, which may have the effect of reducing the adequacy of cash benefits and limiting options for returning to work (Spieler, 2017).

Occupational Health Care

- **Occupational and general health care are not well coordinated**. Workers' compensation systems represent a tiny fraction of overall health care spending and exert almost no influence on general health care reform efforts, yet trends in health care, such as rising costs, affect workers' compensation stakeholders (Barth, 2010).

- **Cost-control measures are imperfect and may reduce quality and access to care**. Workers' compensation lacks effective demand-side cost control due to the provision of no-cost coverage for injured workers (Mueller and Harris, 2010). Alternative measures to control costs, such as fee schedules that cap spending on medical providers, may reduce access to or the quality of benefits by narrowing the population of providers willing to serve injured workers (Grabell and Berkes, 2015b; Spieler, 2017). Limits on injured workers' choice of provider may reduce satisfaction with care (Belton, 2010).

- **Parties disagree on the effectiveness of evidence-based guidelines**. Treatment guidelines may improve the consistency and quality of care, but some stakeholders believe onerous guidelines will lead providers to refuse to serve the workers' compensation population, reducing access to care (Mueller and Harris, 2010).
- **Problems remain in disability determination**. Impairment ratings do not necessarily capture loss of function, and medical care for disabled workers focuses too much on clinical outcomes and too little on functional outcomes (Mueller et al., 2017). One comprehensive analysis found significant variability in maximum compensation for similar injuries across states—while the national average maximum benefit for losing an arm in 2015 was $169,878, state maximums ranged from $48,840 in Alabama to $859,634 in Nevada (Groeger, Grabell, and Cotts, 2015).
- **Disability determination reference guides have limitations**. The evidence base for impairment-rating guides is incomplete across editions of the guides, injury types, injury severity, and individual characteristics (Forst, Friedman, and Chukwu, 2010; Seabury, Neuhauser, and Nuckols, 2013). Changes in ratings guides may reduce benefits for injured workers (Spieler, 2017; Moss et al., 2012).

Workers' Compensation Today

Recent trends in workers' compensation coverage and costs reflect the economic recovery from the 2007–2009 recession and recent state-level regulatory reforms. Total employer costs for workers' compensation rose an estimated 20.1 percent between 2011 and 2015, most of which can be attributed to the expansion of employment: covered wages rose 18.7 percent and covered employment rose 7.7 percent in the same period (McLaren and Baldwin, 2017). While relative costs rose slightly across all states, costs fell in 27 states and rose in 24, and significant cost reductions appear to be related to regulatory changes in state programs.

Another important issue affecting workers' compensation systems is the push in some states to establish alternative arrangements in which employers can design parallel benefit programs for injured workers or forego injured-worker benefits entirely. The degree to which these programs interact with or resemble standard workers' compensation varies widely (Burton, 2017). The only widely adopted alternative to mandatory coverage is the Texas opt-out model, where workers' compensation coverage is voluntary, but employers who forego coverage lose their protection from negligence liability.[2] In some cases, employers who do not purchase workers' compensation insurance may seek liability protection through other means, such as adding arbitration agreements to employment contracts. Other states have explored opt-out

---

[2] Here and elsewhere, we refer to the Texas program as "opt-out," following much of the literature and public commentary on that issue. In fact, the default position in Texas is no coverage, meaning interested employers must "opt-in" to the workers' compensation system.

arrangements that attempted to specify some minimum standards for employee benefits. In 2013, Oklahoma passed a significant reform to its workers' compensation statute that included a clause allowing employers to opt out of workers' compensation if they developed an alternative benefit plan that offered similar indemnity benefits to those provided in Oklahoma's workers' compensation system. However, Oklahoma's opt-out legislation gave employers broad flexibility to define other crucial system features, such as the exclusion of certain health conditions, time limits for reporting, and the use of binding arbitration in place of the workers' compensation court to resolve disputes. In 2016, the opt-out clause was ruled unconstitutional by the Oklahoma Supreme Court because it created radically different legal treatment for otherwise similar individuals in the same class of workers (Szymendera, 2017). A more widely adopted and less radical alternative to such opt-out models is a "carve-out" for specific industries (Levine, Neuhauser, and Petersen, 2002). These arrangements typically allow employees and employers to negotiate alternative workers' compensation systems through a collective bargaining process. Carve-outs tend to focus on procedural aspects of workers' compensation systems, such as dispute resolution and rules regulating legal representation and physician choice.

A related issue to opt-out is whether state laws can deny benefits to certain categories of injured workers but also limit their rights to bring a tort claim against their employer—so-called dual denial. Disputes related to dual denial typically occur in cases where the causality of the injury is in question—in most cases, when injuries or diseases are categorically excluded from workers' compensation benefits, they will also be removed from exclusive remedy protection (Spieler, 2017). Recent research suggests policy reforms in many states in the last two decades have raised the evidentiary standard to prove the work-relatedness of an injury, possibly increasing the possibility of dual denial (Spieler and Burton, 2012). In cases where there is uncertainty about whether work was a major contributory cause (MCC) of the injury or disease, questions remain about whether denial of benefits disqualifies the employer from exclusive remedy protection (Burton, 2017).

Dual denial is viewed by many observers as part of a broader pattern in which workers with injuries related to work do not receive compensation or receive inadequate compensation in the workers' compensation system (Spieler and Burton, 2012). This can occur for several reasons. The rise in employment at temporary staffing and professional employer organizations has created greater uncertainty about who is covered and has excluded some workers from coverage. Temporary workers are covered by workers' compensation but may not understand how to file a claim, while independent contractors are typically exempt from coverage requirements and generally do not have coverage (Utterback, Meyers, and Wurzelbacher, 2014). Workers also may not file claims for some compensable injuries, either because of a lack of understanding of the workers' compensation system, a negative view of the system based on coworker experiences, or fear of illegal employer retaliation (Strunin and Boden, 2004b). For claims that are filed, compensability standards have, in general, become more complex and stringent.

Chapter Three. Stakeholder Views of System Challenges

The critical perspectives sketched in the previous chapter are likely well known to many workers' compensation policymakers and system observers. However, some stakeholder groups may be more vocal or better coordinated than others. For instance, the International Association of Industrial Accident Boards and Commissions (IAIABC) has held discussions about system goals and policy challenges at several of their recent meetings, yet IAIABC membership is centered on state agency staff, claims administrators, and other workers' compensation professionals; workers and employers may be less well represented. NIOSH accordingly requested that RAND explore the beliefs and priorities of multiple stakeholder groups and attempt to identify a synthesis that could be used to identify constructive priorities for workers' compensation policy reforms and for research, evaluation, and translational activities by NIOSH and other research funders.

To keep the scope of the study tractable, RAND selected (with input from NIOSH) five groups of stakeholders and system participants to focus on:

- workers
- employers
- claims administrators
- state agency leaders
- occupational health care providers.

RAND convened separate conference calls with each of these groups between February and April 2018. Nine invitees from each stakeholder group were initially contacted, with additional invitations from alternate lists sent if invitees were not available or were not able to find a mutually agreeable time. Names and affiliations of stakeholder group participants are provided in Appendix A. Participants in each group were provided with a group-specific agenda covering a subset of the topics identified in our review of published critical perspectives. While we tailored the discussion agendas in an attempt to allow more focus on topics where each group might have the greatest expertise, we also requested participants to identify challenges or policy priorities that had been omitted from the group-specific agendas. Discussions were transcribed by a research assistant, and key themes were summarized by one of the coauthors of this report (Broten). Dr. Dworsky then reviewed the summaries along with the full transcripts and led the drafting of this chapter. After an initial draft of the report was completed, one representative from each stakeholder group was invited to review the draft report and provide another round of feedback, with an emphasis on whether major issues were omitted or inaccurately characterized by other stakeholder groups.

In this chapter, we seek to characterize major challenges for workers' compensation policy identified by each stakeholder group, including areas of agreement or disagreement between groups. In the following chapter, we review promising policy solutions identified by stakeholders and also describe research activities or gaps in the evidence base that stakeholders felt would be most useful for improving worker well-being and guiding policymaking.

Overview of Challenges Identified as Major Priorities

Different stakeholder groups raised a wide range of concerns about current workers' compensation system design and performance. The distribution of concerns across stakeholder groups is summarized in Table 3.1, where an "X" indicates that a topic was identified as a major policy challenge. It is important that readers do not interpret the absence of a mark to mean that the topic is *not* perceived as a challenge for that stakeholder group. Limitations on the length and scope of discussions and variation in the discussion agenda across groups meant that not all topics were covered in equivalent depth in all conversations.

Table 3.1: Overview of Workers' Compensation Policy Challenges Identified by Stakeholder Groups

Prevention of Injury and Disability	Workers	Employers	Insurers and Claims Administrators	Health Care Providers	State Agency Leaders
Injury Prevention and Safety Incentives	X			X	
Policies Tailored to Small Employers	X			X	
Disability Prevention/Return-to-Work Programs				X	X
System Coverage, Benefit Adequacy, and Cost Spillovers					
Safety and Coverage for Alternative Work Arrangements	X	X		X	X
Causation, Apportionment, and Coverage of Diseases	X	X	X		
Benefit Adequacy and Cost Spillovers to Social Programs	X				
Claim Management Processes					
Excessive Litigation and Navigation Challenges for Workers	X				X
System Too Focused on Compliance and Cost Control, Not Outcomes			X		X
Data Management and Claim Tracking Problems Within Employers		X			
Occupational Health Care					
Lack of Integration with Rest of Health Care System	X	X	X	X	X
Poor Quality Care: Overtreatment				X	X
Poor Quality Care: Access and Denial of Care	X				
Focus on Quality Improvement, Functional Outcomes				X	

11

The bolded topic headers in Table 3.1 derived from the policy priorities discussed in Chapter Two, whereas specific priorities and suggestions emerged from stakeholder conversations. *Prevention of injury and disability* refers broadly to programs and policies within workers' compensation designed to reduce injury rates and transitions into long-term disability. These include but are not limited to incentive-rating, loss control, and firm-level safety incentive programs, as well as return-to-work and disability management programs. These programs may be administered and financed by state governments, claims administrators, employers, or other independent entities. *System coverage, benefit adequacy, and cost spillovers* refers broadly to the extent to which workers' compensation systems cover costs related to workplace injuries. This includes overall access to coverage preceding an injury, the generosity and appropriateness of benefits during and after the injury, and the long-term societal consequences of workplace injuries. Coverage and benefit adequacy are primarily shaped by state workers' compensation laws but may also be affected by actions taken by employers and claims administrators. *Claim management processes* refers to policies, procedures, and norms within workers' compensation systems that affect the path from injury to closing a claim. These are affected by decisions across stakeholder groups, including state agencies, claims administrators, employers, workers, insurers, physicians, attorneys, and third-party service providers, such as data analysis firms. *Occupational health care* refers primarily to evaluating workers' compensation claims and delivering health services to injured workers. Policy in this area engages most stakeholders and such outside groups as professional associations, research agencies, and evaluation boards.

Limitations

Other stakeholders likely to have valuable insights into system performance were omitted from our conversations due to resource constraints on the project. Stakeholder groups that were considered but were not convened included attorneys, health care providers without a significant occupational medicine focus, health and life insurers (who are the leading providers of private disability insurance), and officials from state and federal programs that have significant interactions with workers' compensation (such as state short-term disability insurance programs, Centers for Medicaid and Medicare Services [CMS], and the Social Security Agency [SSA]).

Participants were nonrandomly selected, with invitation lists drawn largely from contacts of RAND and NIOSH staff, participants in NIOSH's National Occupational Research Agenda Industry Councils, and from referrals by initial invitees. While the research team sought to choose a diverse group of participants for each stakeholder group, there should be no pretense that the viewpoints collected here are representative of all relevant stakeholder group members. The limited sources of information available within the resource constraints of this study limit the diversity of opinion, experience, observations, and recommendations included here.

Furthermore, as noted above, the limited duration and scope of discussions and the variation in the discussion agenda across groups meant that not all topics were addressed in all conversations. Certain topics that are known to be areas of public health and stakeholder concern, such as the limited evidence base on optimal disability determination methods or the impact of job strain on mental health, may have been neglected due to these constraints.[1] Similarly, concerns with certain procedural aspects of workers' compensation policy (such as the frequency of lump-sum settlements in place of ongoing disability benefits) might have received more attention if the study's scope had been sufficient for us to include a group of workers' compensation attorneys. Problems relating to cost spillovers and coordination with other social insurance programs may likewise have been neglected because the relevant agencies were not represented in our discussions.

Prevention of Injury and Disability

Workers, health care providers, and state agency leaders generally agreed that prevention of injury and prevention of disability after injury need to be top priorities for research and workers' compensation policymakers. Discussion with workers focused heavily on the unintended consequences of formal claim-based safety incentives. Other approaches to injury prevention emerged as a theme in several group conversations, as did the need for improved return-to-work and disability-prevention efforts to minimize the functional and economic consequences of those injuries that do occur.

Incentives Based on Workers' Compensation Costs or Injury Rates Have Unintended Consequences

The national commission recognized the encouragement of safety as a central objective of workers' compensation. Incentives for employers to provide safe workplaces can be built into the design of workers' compensation systems, yet stakeholders noted that successful policies in particular jurisdictions have not diffused widely throughout other state systems. A key challenge raised by multiple stakeholder groups was that workers' compensation systems provide strong incentives for cost control but may not directly incentivize safety or good worker outcomes.

In general, the pricing of workers' compensation insurance creates financial incentives for employers and claims administrators to minimize the costs of medical care, indemnity benefits, and administrative, legal, or other loss adjustment costs. Commercially insured employers typically face experience-rating, and large-deductible plans also create incentives for cost control. Larger employers that are more likely to self-insure, meanwhile, bear all the financial

---

[1] Associations between various dimensions of working conditions and depressive symptoms have been convincingly documented in observational studies (Theorell et al., 2015). We suspect that mental health was not emphasized in our discussions in part because many mental disorders have been effectively removed from workers' compensation systems by increasing evidentiary standards.

risk associated with workers' compensation claims and thus should have even stronger incentives to limit claim costs.

Unfortunately, stakeholders raised concerns that these financial incentives for cost control do not necessarily result in improved safety. Concerns were voiced about the consequences of incentives for workers and managers to minimize specific measures of injury rates, such as workers' compensation claims or injuries meeting the recording criteria of the Occupational Safety and Health Administration (OSHA). A union representative for workers in large manufacturing plants described a pair of factories owned and operated by the same employer and building the same product with essentially the same production process: one factory has numerous workers' compensation claims for soft-tissue injuries, while the other typically has no compensable injuries. The union representative viewed this pattern as an illustration of reporting differences driven by the degree to which managers respond to safety incentives created by corporate management: the plant manager, the safety department, and the corporate-level managers track OSHA-recordable and workers' compensation claims as performance indicators. However, reductions in recordable or compensable injuries did not reflect safety improvements; instead, managers in one jurisdiction were encouraging workers to report claims to the union's sickness and accident fund, which is not treated as a performance indicator for management.

Employers did not entirely agree with the characterization of incentive-based safety programs as prone to unintended consequences. They asserted that OSHA's "whistleblower memo" of 2012 had deterred employers from providing financial incentives that would effectively penalize workers who raised safety concerns or reported injuries.[2] That said, any pullback from formal safety incentive programs would not necessarily imply the absence of other, less tangible managerial incentives to distort record keeping. Worker advocates raised questions about whether an employer's safety record reflects actual safety or systematic underreporting of cases where work-relatedness is unclear.

Safety Interventions Were Viewed as More Promising Than Incentive Programs and Less Likely to Create Incentives for Underreporting

Stakeholders generally were more supportive of injury prevention and disability management programs than of financial incentives (such as experience-rating) based on claim costs. Financial incentives based on loss costs or reported injury rates attempt to incentivize outcomes but are limited by the fact that the intended outcomes are imperfectly related to the ultimate objective of improved worker health and safety: both loss costs and injury rates can be reduced by manipulating injury reporting.

---

[2] Occupational Health and Safety Administration, 2012. The effect of the whistleblower memo on the use of safety incentives has not, to our knowledge, been rigorously evaluated.

In contrast, injury prevention and disability management programs offer a way to avoid the measurement and reporting problems raised by experience-rating or other outcome-based incentives by rewarding processes that are anticipated (or, ideally, proven) to promote worker health and safety.

Several stakeholder groups noted the challenges that small employers can face in developing and implementing safety improvements, in particular a lack of expertise and technical resources. Small employers are often exempt from experience-rating, so reliance on price signals or other incentives based directly on safety records may not even be applicable to the smallest employers. Stakeholders, including both occupational health care providers and worker representatives, identified several examples of successful programs in which workers' compensation insurers work with employers—including small employers—on safety improvement, specifically the Ohio Bureau of Workers' Compensation (BWC) Safety Intervention Grant program and the Certificate of Recognition (COR) program operated by WorkSafeBC, British Columbia's provincial workers' compensation fund. We discuss these examples in greater detail in the next chapter since further study and expansion of these models might be a priority.

Inadequate Investment in Disability Prevention After Injury

A related concern voiced by numerous stakeholders was a lack of attention to secondary and tertiary prevention, or disability prevention, after the occurrence of an injury. State agency leaders—including some from states widely viewed as having developed successful return-to-work interventions—clearly identified return-to-work outcomes as a top priority for workers' compensation policy. Specific barriers were identified as standing in the way of improved return-to-work policies, including the availability of financing, resistance to reform by intermediaries or "cottage industries" that had evolved to address other system problems, and employer attitudes. We discuss disability prevention at greater length below in several places. Stakeholders identified major problems with claim management processes and health care delivery, which we discuss later in this chapter. They also identified many proven or promising policy changes, which we discuss in Chapter Four.

System Coverage, Benefit Adequacy, and Cost Spillovers

Workers and employers highlighted numerous concerns about problems involved in defining the boundaries of the workers' compensation system.

Coverage of Alternative Work Arrangements

Worker advocates noted that workers in alternative work arrangements—such as temporary-agency workers, contract workers, or independent contractors—are often denied coverage. Even when covered by workers' compensation, worker advocates noted that these workers are significantly more likely to be injured, even after adjusting for short job tenure, echoing recent research findings (Foley, 2017; Zaidman, 2017). Some employers also agreed that safety practices and claims administration for temporary and contract workers tended to lag behind procedures for direct hires. As one worker advocate noted, "[T]he real fundamental issue is that the temp agency does not control the work process, and is not at the work site—so why do they have the workers' comp policy?" Other employers, however (including a representative from a high-hazard industry), indicated that they already have rigorous processes in place for hiring and orientating contract employees but that such efforts were costly and were unlikely to be pursued by smaller host employers.

Coverage of Conditions: Work-Relatedness and Causation

Participants cited many examples where work-related injuries were undercovered or coverage was denied due to apportionment, causation standards, or time-to-first-claim rules. Examples included soft-tissue injuries at auto plants, asthma, and silicosis.

Worker advocates expressed the view that debates around apportionment and causation are typically driven by a desire to deny claims or reduce coverage, not simply a desire for fairness. Claims administrators and physicians also raised concerns about the state of the evidence base for determining causation and apportionment.

Underreporting of Injuries

Worker advocates emphasized that underreporting of injuries by workers is a widespread problem, particularly for low-wage workers who may feel vulnerable to retaliation or who may attach a sense of stigma to claiming workers' compensation:

> In our society, there is a belief that if someone goes on workers' comp, they hurt themselves and they are to blame. . . . A lot of workers will stay out of the workers' comp system because they feel that they will be blamed, ridiculed and shunned by others.

There is concern that vulnerable worker populations underreport injuries irrespective of stigma. A 2009 study on low-wage workers commissioned by the National Employment Law Project found that only 8 percent of low-wage workers with a serious injury on the job filed a workers' compensation claim (Bernhardt et al., 2009). Illegal retaliatory actions by the employer were reported to be common. Health care providers also noted that underreporting of injuries is especially pronounced among workers receiving treatment from federally qualified health centers (FQHCs), since workers can obtain care (and the health care providers can obtain reimbursement) without filing an insurance claim. Underreporting by health care providers was also felt to reflect a poor understanding of workers' compensation processes and occupational health care concerns in the broader health care system, a theme that we discuss further below.

Inadequate Benefits and Cost Spillovers to Other Social and Health Insurance Programs

Some worker advocates expressed a sense of frustration that cost-control efforts, especially laws narrowing coverage of specific diseases or injuries, had begun to undermine the mutually beneficial nature of the grand bargain. Worker advocates cited egregious examples of claims that were denied based on apportionment despite long work histories with clear disease-specific occupational exposures. Faith in the no-fault nature of the system—which was highlighted by an employer participant as a great system advantage—appears to be wearing thin among some worker advocates. As one worker advocate put it, "[T]hese big employers . . . really do feel the work-related injuries are the workers' fault as opposed to unsafe conditions." Speaking about apportionment, another worker advocate viewed legislative debates as being driven by a desire to "build in more excuses to deny claims."

Claims administrators also noted more generally that efforts by states to lower business costs have led to underreporting and more exclusions and that these efforts were often self-defeating because they sometimes lead to more severe health problems and higher future costs for employers and society as a whole. Workers felt that inadequate benefits and cost spillovers onto other social and health insurance programs severely undermined safety incentives while placing strains on important safety net programs. Cost spillovers to federal programs, in particular, were felt to facilitate a race to the bottom between states with respect to coverage and benefit generosity. Claims administrators agreed with workers that the race to the bottom was a dynamic that had led to counterproductive policymaking in many jurisdictions.

The generosity and adequacy of permanent disability benefits for approved claims received less attention in our discussions than concerns about coverage of workers and exclusions of claims. State agency leaders cautioned that building national consensus around standards of benefit adequacy or approaches to compensating permanent disabilities might be difficult due to the wide variety of approaches taken by different states to determining disability benefits; those stakeholders felt that efforts to prevent injury and disability were more politically feasible since such efforts, if successful, can simultaneously improve worker OSH and produce cost savings for employers. However, some worker advocates raised the point that the exclusion of certain types of damages other than earnings losses from the workers' compensation system should be revisited. One worker advocate highlighted the risk that workers' families face of losing fringe benefits, such as dependent health care coverage, in the event of employment losses. The idea of providing compensation for functional and quality-of-life losses in addition to earnings losses was also raised in our conversation with worker advocates. As we discuss in Chapter Four, more rigorous evidence on the consequences of injury and illness could help policymakers judge whether compensation for these other forms of losses could be built into the workers' compensation system without dramatically increasing system complexity.

Claim Management Processes

Stakeholders were also concerned about system complexity and the frequency of disputes in the workers' compensation process.

Too Litigious and Difficult to Navigate for Workers, Small Employers

Stakeholder groups agreed widely that excessive litigation and excessively contentious dispute resolution mechanisms were deleterious not only to system efficiency and cost control but to the health and economic outcomes of workers themselves.

Some state agency leaders pointed out that litigation and complex disputes are concentrated in a relatively small proportion of cases where causation or other coverage issues are unclear. There was some hope that wider adoption of presumptions backed by epidemiological evidence could help to reduce disputes, but several state agency leaders responded that presumptions, in their experience, had not reduced the likelihood of litigation.

One state agency leader argued that growing litigation volumes were an unintended consequence of an excessive focus on cost containment, both through the proliferation of formal cost-control processes (which generally must provide opportunities for appeal to preserve due process and avoid high-cost errors) and through changes to coverage (such as apportionment or MCC standards) that increased the volume of marginal cases subject to disputes. One state agency head indicated that cost containment expenses paid to intermediaries (such as utilization review contractors) had, ironically, become a problematic cost driver in their own right.

Employers also raised concerns about litigation and inefficient dispute resolution. One issue that was raised was that complex workers' compensation cases sometimes occur concurrently with other disputes between workers and employers, such as a discrimination case. In these cases, overlapping legal proceedings and the involvement of separate groups within the company can make it more difficult for the worker to return to work. Meanwhile, claims administrators noted that small employers often had difficulty navigating the claims and return-to-work processes.

In general, worker advocates felt that workers' compensation systems in most states had become too complex for workers to navigate without legal representation. Yet workers also pointed out that many states have restricted legal fees, making it difficult for some workers to obtain representation. Worker advocates noted that applicants' attorneys sometimes take on unmanageable caseloads (perhaps 100 to 200 active cases per attorney) in states with excessively restrictive fee schedules, making it difficult for attorneys to serve as effective advocates. Conversely, employers pointed out that attorneys sometimes have strong financial incentives to maximize disability benefits for workers and may accordingly give workers advice that undermines return to work.

Different problems confront workers who lack representation. For these workers, lack of confidence in their ability to navigate the workers' compensation system can create a barrier that exacerbates other barriers to claiming: a worker advocate noted, "[T]he primary advocate for the injured worker is the physician or health care provider. And in general, they don't have training to deal with this. . . . [T]he worker advocacy part is being done by people who don't know the system and are discouraged from really working well in the system. The system is so stacked against workers that it is surprising that they actually get through it." We discuss stakeholder interest in better training and case management as a priority for policy evaluation in the next chapter.

Focus on Compliance Leads to Complexity and Distracts from Other Objectives

Employers and claims administrators felt that workers' compensation systems sometimes emphasized compliance with workers' compensation regulations to the exclusion of other objectives. In addition, multistate employers can find it challenging to comply with system rules in multiple states. State agencies also cautioned that claims administrators sometimes created barriers to productive return-to-work planning, impeding direct communication between the worker, the physician, and the employer. An agency leader from a state with a well-regarded stay-at-work program emphasized the importance of early direct contact and clear communication with employers.

Data Management and Claim Tracking Problems Within Employers

Employers felt that workers were harmed by poor coordination between different safety, wellness, and benefit programs within employers. Safety management, worker wellness, nonoccupational disability benefits, sick leave, and leave provided under the Family Medical Leave Act (FMLA) were all named as examples of processes that might have separate record-keeping systems, preventing relevant information from feeding back into prevention efforts. For example, one employer noted that their OSHA reporting software tracked days of work absence, but their workers' compensation software did not. Another employer said they have difficulty conforming OSHA and workers' compensation data tracking because OSHA reports are based on the date of injury, while the workers' compensation system tracks date of claim. (In complex cases, such as occupational diseases, these are not the same.) In addition, different parts of an employer's management team may focus on narrowly defined objectives. Safety prevention systems and workers' compensation systems are insufficiently integrated, in one employer's words, because safety administrators think "the horse is out of the barn" once an incident is reported.

Occupational Health Care

Concerns about delivery and quality of occupational health care were a central theme of all stakeholder conversations.

Lack of Integration with Other Health Care

Across all stakeholder groups, the fragmentation of health care delivery between workers' compensation and other health care payers and providers was the most widely cited challenge to the health and well-being of injured workers. Employers felt that poor communication and the fragmentation of health records between occupational and nonoccupational health care providers harmed patients.

Confusion about privacy and information sharing may amplify the consequences of care fragmentation between group health and workers' compensation. Employers noted that many medical professionals worry about Health Insurance Portability and Accountability Act (HIPAA) compliance when contacted by a provider in the workers' compensation system, even though communications would be from medical professional to medical professional. Similarly, doctors may mistakenly think that sharing with the workers' compensation insurer creates new HIPAA problems.

As another example of barriers that can hinder effective treatment and return to work, a health care provider cited a Montana Supreme Court decision holding that ex parte communications between treating physicians and claims administrators violated a right to privacy guaranteed in the Montana constitution. While communications between physicians and claims administrators are still allowed with patient consent, the decision was seen as having a strong chilling effect on provider involvement in disability management and return to work: "[P]roviders will not even communicate with employers about the ability to accommodate injured workers, which effectively disables the concept of prevention in occupational medicine."

Problems Due to Lack of Medical Management/Population Health/Comorbidities

Multiple stakeholder groups raised concerns about the inability of workers' compensation systems to address worker health and nonoccupational comorbidities before a claim is filed. This approach might be adequate for traumatic, acute injuries, but for chronic conditions, those with lifestyle factors or cumulative risks, or occupational diseases, this fragmentation of care was viewed as a major problem. Claims administrators noted that this is even a problem for acute injuries if they are exacerbated by comorbidities.

Both employers and health care providers pointed out that workers' compensation medical care is distinguished sharply from other parts of the health care system by its explicit orientation toward return to work and functional improvement, so the failure to engage with occupational health providers before a workers' compensation claim is filed was viewed as a missed opportunity. Even though functional improvement and participation in the activities of daily living are widely acknowledged as goals of the health care system, discussion participants felt that occupational providers tended to be more focused on these objectives in comparison to other health care providers. Health insurers are likely to underinvest in prevention and medical management activities that result in savings for workers' compensation insurers, since the health insurers may not reap the full financial benefits of chronic disease management.

Claims administrators also raised concerns about the extent to which worker health (including comorbidities and poor health behaviors, such as smoking) made injuries more difficult to treat once they occurred. Self-insured firms have the potential to internalize this externality, but we heard concerns raised that poor integration between workers' compensation and other medical care prevented this.

Poor-Quality Care

Consistent with published critiques, there was widespread concern among discussion participants about the quality of care provided in workers' compensation systems (Franklin et al., 2015). As with the U.S. health care system more broadly, concerns about overtreatment and provision of low-value care coexisted with concerns about undertreatment and insufficient access to care.

Undertreatment and Denial of Appropriate Care

Workers raised concerns about system features that tend, in practice, to deny timely medical care to injured workers. Texas, the only state where any employer can unconditionally opt out of workers' compensation and offer voluntary workplace injury benefits with minimal state oversight, was held out by workers as a polar example of systems that are deliberately designed to control costs by denying care and compensation to injured workers. Worker advocates expressed serious concern that opt-out plans represent an erosion of the grand bargain and tend to have design features that disadvantage workers. Some employers, meanwhile, expressed support for alternative dispute-resolution mechanisms, such as the arbitration procedures frequently used in opt-out plans. We discuss models for alternative dispute resolution in the next chapter.

Furthermore, disputed claims can affect access to needed care, undermining the benefits of a no-fault system. Concerns were raised about delay and denial of care in disputed cases. In some cases, workers felt that problems originated with health care providers; examples were cited of medical providers who tell injured workers to come back with a lawyer, instead of providing treatment.

Overtreatment and Provision of Inappropriate Care

Conversely, health care providers also expressed concerns that poor-quality care persists in workers' compensation because some payers are too deferential to treating physicians: one participant stated that "most workers' compensation adjudicators feel like they have no authority and no legal basis to argue with a doctor about doing most things." Even in systems such as California or Washington where evidence-based guidelines have been in place for some time, physicians indicated that payers and claims adjudicators lacked sufficient understanding of the guidelines to apply them with confidence. Participants indicated that adoption of clinical guidelines was necessary but not sufficient to produce high-quality care: systems also need procedures to remove providers who are bad apples, and an adjudication process that is capable of applying the guidelines with confidence is also necessary. In the absence of such understanding, the claims management process is heavily dependent on an ecosystem of contractors specializing in such functions as utilization review or case management. The financial incentives of these intermediaries may not be oriented toward the promotion of high-quality care or worker outcomes.

The Opioid Crisis

Care provided through workers' compensation is now acknowledged to have contributed meaningfully to the United States' opioid epidemic (Franklin et al., 2005). Employers also felt that opioid overprescribing was a symptom of the broader problem of care fragmentation and lack of information sharing between workers' compensation and other parts of the health care system. Apart from the risks of addiction and overdose, early opioid prescribing has been shown to exacerbate disability and increase time away from work, which can place workers at greater risk of job loss and economic hardship. Such policy solutions as the adoption of workers' compensation formularies and stronger requirements for the use of prescription drug monitoring programs were suggested as promising directions by employers.

Payment Reform and Quality Improvement

Health care providers suggested that workers would benefit from a focus on quality improvement and applying better standards of care. Particular attention was paid to measuring and incentivizing outcomes beyond return to work. Restoration of function was identified as an important but neglected goal for health systems, both in workers' compensation and more broadly. Health care providers asserted that the health care system generally does not track patient function (as opposed to pathology or symptoms). Better measurement of function could also help support the expansion of workers' compensation benefits to cover noneconomic losses or broader functional losses in addition to earnings losses, an objective identified by workers.

At present, however, stakeholders felt that the health care system was not effective in promoting either functional improvement or return to work. One state agency leader even suggested that medical providers can play too much of a role in determining if the injured worker is ready to return to work in workers' compensation. The concern is that health care providers who are not trained or equipped to manage the return-to-work process may tend to err on the side of higher disability duration to allow medical recovery while ignoring the risk of poor disability and functional outcomes associated with longer spells out of work. In general, the health care system is not designed to handle issues that arise between workers and their employers regarding facilitation or modification.

Political Economy and Workers' Compensation Reform

As noted by Rick Victor, a system feature that has helped to make workers' compensation politically viable for over a century is the functioning of the political system to reach effective compromises between the interests of workers and employers (Victor, 2018). If an imbalance arises between the political power of workers and business, the grand bargain may become less sustainable. The current political climate in many states might appear to pose major constraints on the direction of short-term workers' compensation reform efforts. As Emily Spieler wrote in 2017,

> While some stakeholders are attempting to improve the dialogue, there is little evidence as yet that this will heal the deep distrust that exists on all sides. The political campaigns to reduce costs for employers—irrespective of the effects on workers—are likely to continue. . . . At best, there is an uneasy equilibrium. At worst, successful attacks on the program will further erode its reach. The aggregate costs will continue to go down, masking the increasing transfer of costs associated with occupational illness and injury to workers and other benefit programs. (Spieler, 2017)

Despite these political constraints apparent under the status quo, many system participants, including both employers and workers, remain committed to improving the workers' compensation system. In the following chapter, we examine policies and research needs identified by stakeholders in greater detail.

Chapter Four. Policy Options and Research Needs

In the context of the above suggestions for prioritization, we use this chapter to present some examples of successful policies that were suggested by stakeholders as models warranting expansion or more careful evaluation and attention from policymakers. We also highlight certain research needs that were identified as high priorities given current gaps in the evidence base and the potential to inform major system improvements.

Multiple stakeholder groups suggested that NIOSH could play an important role in identifying and suggesting best practices for state workers' compensation systems. Stakeholders also identified gaps in the more basic evidence base on occupational health, injury prevention, disability prevention, return to work, and cost spillovers, including specific areas where NIOSH and other research sponsors could strongly affect policy.

One notable feature of the conversations was that several stakeholder groups expressed limited interest in either the federalization of workers' compensation or the establishment of minimum standards by the federal government. This might seem surprising given that stakeholders also lamented the race to the bottom in terms of coverage and benefits, but even some stakeholders who might be expected to support a stronger federal role felt that the deep-rooted historical independence and diversity of state systems made it unconstructive to even discuss federal standards, let alone a federal role in benefit financing. Some worker advocates, however, did argue that greater federal oversight would be necessary to stop the race to the bottom. One suggestion was for the Department of Labor (DOL) to resume monitoring of state-level program changes.

While stakeholders other than workers did not seem eager to establish formal federal standards for state workers' compensation policies, many participants expressed the hope that the federal government, and NIOSH in particular, could take a more active role in developing and disseminating guidelines and best practices for the design, operation, and financing of workers' compensation systems. Health care providers noted that NIOSH lacks the authority to address workers' compensation system challenges through regulation. As a public health agency, however, NIOSH could be instrumental in improving injury and disability prevention and supporting quality improvement in occupational health care. State agency heads, meanwhile, suggested that NIOSH might select policy topics for study by considering what areas of system design are most likely to achieve consensus on the need for national standards. Claims administrators suggested that federal research and guidance identifying best practices for contentious areas of workers' compensation (such as causation, claims administration, and occupational disease presumptions) would be welcomed by many stakeholders. Given that state agencies and claims administrators were particularly dismissive of any suggested policies that even resembled federalization, it is notable that they nonetheless identified a valuable role for NIOSH and federal research funders.

Policy Priorities

Table 4.1 summarizes policy and research priorities identified by specific stakeholder groups. An "X" indicates that the discussion group identified the policy area or research need as a priority, but the absence of a mark does not imply the reverse. Time limitations on discussions oriented conversations toward those issues most closely related to each stakeholder group's roles within workers' compensation systems.

Table 4.1: Policy Options and Research Needs Identified by Stakeholder Groups

Policy Options Warranting Wider Adoption or Further Study	Workers	Employers	Insurers/Claims Administrators	Health Care Providers	State Agency Leaders
Removing Barriers to Claiming and System Navigation	X		X	X	X
Injury and Disability Prevention Programs	X	X	X	X	X
Improving Occupational Health Care Delivery	X			X	X
Integration with Rest of Health Care System	X	X	X	X	X
Improvement in Health Records, Communication, and Education		X		X	
Research Needs					
Causation of Occupational Diseases and Disability Outcomes	X	X	X		
Identification of Best Practices and Optimal System Features		X	X	X	
Models for Improving Dispute Resolution	X	X			X
Cost Shifting to Social Programs and Families	X				
Impacts of Changing Work Arrangements	X	X		X	

Removing Barriers to Claiming and System Navigation

Claims administrators suggested that evidence on best practices for the rules of a workers' compensation system should be compiled and disseminated by an independent party, such as NIOSH. For example, states differ widely in terms of responsibilities and processes for initiating claims, and some arrangements lead to "friction points" that can cause delays in treatment and disability management problems. Access to timely medical care during the period when a claim is pending was also identified as a concern by workers. One proposed solution to this problem is statutory language allowing injured workers to receive care immediately even if a claim is disputed. Maine was identified as a state with helpful statutory provisions guaranteeing access to care (see Spieler, 2017).

Meanwhile, efforts to make the system more navigable for small employers were identified as a promising policy innovation. For example, Oregon's State Accident Insurance Fund (SAIF, a competitive state fund) operates a service center for small employers, and this was viewed as important to SAIF's mission of ensuring affordability and availability of coverage to Oregon businesses.

Injury and Disability Prevention Programs

State agency leaders suggested that a focus on the improvement of worker return-to-work outcomes would be a more fruitful path to system improvement, with greater buy-in from both workers and employers, than efforts to preserve benefit adequacy or make marginal improvements to system processes. The effectiveness of vocational rehabilitation and the efficiency of different models for vocational rehabilitation service delivery were also identified as areas in need of more research.

Stakeholders identified multiple examples of states that have developed and implemented programs that have successfully promoted injury prevention and disability prevention. As part of a broader effort toward identifying best practices and optimal system design, research and guidance on the scalability or generalizability of these successful models would be welcomed by stakeholders. For the convenience of readers unfamiliar with these programs, we provide brief overviews below and identify potential strengths and limitations of these programs as candidates for wider adoption.

One example is the Safety Intervention Grant (SIG) program operated by the Ohio BWC. The SIG program provides eligible employers with three-to-one matching funds to establish engineering controls intended to improve workplace safety. BWC consultants work with employers to determine eligibility and, if needed, to help identify appropriate interventions. The SIG program is administered by the BWC Division of Safety and Hygiene (DSH). The primary funding stream for DSH operations and SIG matching funds is an assessment on workers' compensation premiums (Ohio Bureau of Workers' Compensation, 2017). A peer-reviewed evaluation of the SIG program by researchers from NIOSH and BWC found that participating employers experienced dramatic reductions in both injury rates and costs per claim (Wurzelbacher et al., 2014).

Another example cited was the COR program operated by WorkSafeBC, British Columbia's provincial workers' compensation fund. COR is a voluntary program through which employers can establish injury prevention, injury management, or return-to-work programs. Employers seeking certification are responsible for establishing safety or return-to-work programs that comply with detailed guidelines. They develop these programs in collaboration with an organization known as the "certifying partner," which may be an industry-based safety association. After the programs have been established, the employer arranges for an audit to assess whether the program complies with standards set out by WorkSafeBC.

Although WorkSafeBC is an exclusive workers' compensation insurer for the province, the COR program involves a relatively modest degree of direct involvement by WorkSafeBC and so might offer a more promising model than the Ohio SIG program for states with competitive workers' compensation markets. WorkSafeBC's involvement in the COR process involves the selection and oversight of certifying partners and standards and tools for the COR audit process. Beginning in the year following certification of the programs, employers receive rebates on their workers' compensation premiums. These rebates are substantial: a 10-percent reduction in premiums for a certified safety program and an additional 5-percent reduction for a certified return-to-work program (WorkSafeBC, 2011).

WorkSafeBC provides financial support for the administrative expenses of certifying partners, but training activities and audits are financed by individual employers or industry safety associations. Certifying partner administrative expenses are funded out of an assessment on all employers covered by WorkSafeBC. Rebates to COR recipients are financed by premiums at the industry level, meaning that program participants are effectively cross-subsidized by nonparticipating employers in the same industry (WorkSafeBC, 2011).

A third model for disability prevention and return-to-work promotion has been adopted in Oregon (the Employer-at-Injury Program [EAIP]). Related models have been implemented in other states, including Washington and North Dakota (Ben-Shalom et al., 2017). These programs focus on promoting early return to work by subsidizing and facilitating light-duty or transitional work assignments that allow an injured worker and employer to shorten the duration of total disability and remain engaged with work. Oregon's EAIP illustrates the basic design of these programs. The target population consists of workers' compensation claimants with work restrictions that interfere with their regular jobs. The intervention consists of wage subsidies, funding for worksite modification or equipment purchases up to $5,000, or funding for minor skill development.[1]

Oregon also has a wage subsidy program known as the Preferred Worker Program (PWP), which encourages new employers to hire workers whose work limitations prevent them from returning to their jobs at injury. Benefits in the PWP are similar to those in the EAIP, with a somewhat more generous allowance for worksite modification; in addition to the wage subsidy, PWP pays for workers' compensation premiums and any costs of a new claim filed by the disabled worker for the first three years after hire.[2] The EAIP is administered by the workers'

---

[1] Oregon DCBS Workers' Compensation Division, 2018a.

[2] Oregon DCBS Workers' Compensation Division, 2018c.

compensation insurer, while the PWP is administered by Oregon's workers' compensation agency (the Workers' Compensation Division [WCD] in the Department of Consumer and Business Services [DCBS]). Wage subsidies, interventions, and (in the PWP) workers' compensation premium exemptions and claim costs are financed from the Workers' Benefit Fund, which is supported by a statewide assessment on wages. Interested employers also pay a nominal application fee.[3]

Other programs discussed below, including Washington's Center for Occupational Health Excellence (COHE) model and the New York State Occupational Health Clinic Network (NYS OHCN) model, also have important disability prevention functions; we defer on addressing them until later in this chapter because these interventions are centered on health care delivery.

Unanswered Questions About Injury and Disability Prevention Programs

It is important to note that both Ohio's SIG program and the WorkSafeBC's COR program of successful injury prevention programs have developed in jurisdictions with exclusive state funds (or provincial accident boards). As discussed by Wurzelbacher et al. (2014), insurers in competitive workers' compensation markets may find it more difficult to recoup investments in safety programs, since workers' compensation policies typically have a one-year contract length. Even though the estimates in Wurzelbacher et al. (2014) suggest that a program similar to the Ohio SIG program would be cost-effective for a private workers' compensation insurer even within a one-year time horizon, policyholder turnover inherently creates positive externalities from each insurer's point of view, likely resulting in underinvestment in safety equipment and other interventions that would pay off over a longer period of time.

More broadly, myopic decisionmaking by some small employers (in terms of overestimating the cost of accommodation while excessively discounting the cost of turnover) was cited by one state agency representative as a barrier to socially efficient levels of accommodation. One might observe a similar pattern if these businesses faced high borrowing costs or sharp liquidity constraints. It is also worth noting that moral hazard among small employers who are exempt from experience-rating could also play a role in undermining incentives for accommodation: one state agency leader noted that state efforts to engage small businesses in developing model return-to-work programs had generated insufficient interest among small employers, since most small employers rarely have workers' compensation claims.

If, for whatever reason, employers are unwilling to make cost-effective investments in the accommodation, retention, and recruitment of disabled workers, the provision of even relatively low levels of outside financing or return-to-work coordination might lead to significant improvements in return to work or employment at new jobs. The EAIP and PWP in Oregon, for

---

[3] For financing details, see Oregon DCBS Workers' Compensation Division, 2018b; Oregon DCBS Workers' Compensation Division, 2018d.

example, are funded out of a statewide payroll assessment (currently at 2.8 cents per hour worked for all workers).

The highly structured oversight mechanisms built into the WorkSafeBC COR program also highlight a potential barrier to the adoption of these programs in jurisdictions with weak or underresourced state workers' compensation agencies. State agencies voiced skepticism about the effectiveness of for-profit return-to-work consultants and similar "cottage industries," noting that they are incentivized to maximize profits by contracting with employers but that they may not be very effective at achieving return to work. WorkSafeBC has addressed this problem by defining very clear standards and multitiered certification and auditing procedures for the COR partners.

Lack of awareness of these models by state policymakers may be one barrier to more widespread adoption, suggesting that NIOSH could play a role in dissemination, technical assistance to states, or as a policy clearinghouse. One potential model for such efforts is the State Exchange on Employment and Disability (SEED), a partnership between the Department of Labor Office of Disability Employment Policy (DOL ODEP) and state government organizations (such as the National Council of State Legislatures [NCSL] and the Council of State Governments [CSG]) that has made information about state policies to promote employment of people with disabilities far more accessible. DOL ODEP and its SEED partners also provide technical assistance to state legislatures on legislation affecting people with disabilities. Although there is a degree of overlap between the missions of DOL ODEP and NIOSH with respect to return to work, promoting accommodation, and functional improvement, NIOSH may be uniquely well suited among federal agencies to provide detailed guidance focused on workers' compensation and occupational health, particularly when it comes to issues of health care delivery and injury prevention.

Incentives to Improve Worker Outcomes

Among multiple stakeholder groups, system changes that would prioritize worker outcomes (either through process modifications or directly through pay-for-performance incentives) were viewed as an interesting direction for workers' compensation policymakers to consider. For instance, an expansion of disability benefits to provide more long-term, partial disability benefits (or wage insurance for workers who transition to lower-paying jobs) could give insurers and (experience-rated) employers more skin in the game with respect to helping workers return to work and remain employed in the long run. We note that current proposals to mandate experience-rated long-term disability insurance as a method to reduce transitions to disability have essentially the same motivation of creating a vehicle through which employers and insurers are held financially accountable for preventable disability and entry onto federal disability programs (Autor and Duggan, 2010; U.S. Government Accountability Office, 2018).

Any beneficial incentive effects of such a change would need to be weighed against the risk of additional disputes or any lost benefits of claim closure for workers (Hyatt, 2010).

Furthermore, incentives tied to workers' subsequent employment and disability program participation would need to be risk-adjusted carefully to avoid exacerbating hiring and wage discrimination against older workers and those with visible disabilities. Even if the current political climate makes such a dramatic expansion of benefits unlikely, there may also be opportunities for payment reform in occupational health care that would strengthen incentives for functional improvement and return to work among health care providers.

A greater emphasis on functional measurement and improvement throughout health care was identified as a promising direction for workers' compensation research and policy by health care providers, while the more widespread measurement of function would also be instrumental for the goal identified by workers of modifying benefits to cover loss of function or nonwork disability. This mirrors calls in the research literature for evaluations of the construct validity of impairment guides (Forst, Friedman, and Chukwu, 2010) and evidence that integrated approaches to functional evaluation, such as those implemented in Colorado, can lead to good outcomes for injured workers without raising costs (Bruns, Mueller, and Warren, 2012).

Priorities for Occupational Health Care Delivery

Multiple stakeholders identified both the COHE model and NYS OHCN as leading examples of innovative models for quality improvement and occupational health delivery.

Alternative Models for Occupational Health Care Delivery and Disability Management

The COHE system in Washington State is recognized as a national leader in improving the quality of occupational health care and improving return-to-work outcomes for injured workers. In general, the COHE model can be thought of as a two-pronged intervention. At the community or health-system level, COHEs pursue quality improvement efforts targeted on occupational health care delivery, claims management, and return-to-work efforts. At the level of individual injured workers, COHEs provide health services coordinators to promote coordination among health care providers, employers, workers, and the many other parties involved in workers' compensation claims. COHEs build on existing health systems and must observe standards and practices defined by the Washington Department of Labor and Industries (L&I)—which functions as both the workers' compensation agency and an exclusive state fund for insured employers. COHE services are thus financed by payments from L&I for administrative expenses and for patient-level services (Stapleton and Christian, 2016).

An evaluation of COHE found substantial reductions in long-term disability and claim costs, with synergistic effects between case management and provider adherence to best practices (Wickizer et al., 2011). This is a rare success story in occupational health care delivery, so the COHE model has attracted widespread attention within workers' compensation circles and from federal policymakers as a template for reducing the overall burden of disability (Stapleton and Christian, 2016).

30

A different approach to occupational health care delivery is taken in NYS OHCN. NYS OHCN specializes in diagnosis and care for occupational diseases and environmental exposures, providing workers with access to expertise that may be scarce in other primary care settings. The clinics are accessible (with care provided on a sliding-fee basis) to anyone with a potentially work-related illness, and they also provide group screenings to populations of workers exposed to increased disease risk from workplace exposures. The clinics also serve a research function, producing clinical practice reviews intended to help clinicians provide effective diagnosis and appropriate treatment for occupational diseases and musculoskeletal disorders.

NYS OHCN was widely recognized among stakeholders as a successful model for the provision of occupational health care. NYS OHCN is managed by the state department of public health (the New York Department of Health [NY DOH]) and is partially funded out of the administrative budget of the state workers' compensation agency (the Workers' Compensation Board [WCB]), which in turn is funded by an assessment on workers' compensation premiums. Clinic fees for individual patients seeking treatment for symptomatic diseases are largely paid by workers' compensation, while group screenings are overwhelmingly financed by employers (NYS OHCN, 2017).

Unfortunately, challenges with funding appear to have constrained NYS OHCN from realizing its full potential and expanding its scope of services into such potentially valuable areas as disability management, case coordination, or return-to-work efforts (as in the COHE model). A 2012 report by a state oversight committee noted that although the clinic network has been successful and provides high-quality care, its ability to serve patients has been hampered by inadequate funding, which remained constant in nominal terms at approximately $6 million per year between 1997 and 2009 (New York State Occupational Health Clinics Oversight Committee, 2012).

As noted above in connection with the safety intervention models developed in Ohio and British Columbia, further innovation and greater political commitment may be needed to develop scalable and sustainable financing models for occupational health delivery interventions in states that do not have exclusive state funds. NYS OHCN's funding challenges are not encouraging in this regard. We conjecture that the complexity of NYS OHCN's management structure (in which NY DOH oversees the clinic network and submits budget requests to be funded by WCB out of a larger administrative assessment and then disburses funds to local clinic partners that may have their own overhead requirements) may contribute to NYS OHCN's funding challenges, but more careful study is needed to determine if this is the case.

Concerns were also raised by a health care provider that quality improvement or specialty occupational health similar to that of COHE and NYS OHCN may not generalize to heavily rural states where there are few dedicated occupational health care providers. The NYS OHCN system includes several clinics in largely rural regions, but travel times to metropolitan areas or supporting institutions may be far greater in some midwestern or western states than in the Northeast, leaving the generalizability of the NYS OHCN approach unclear. Furthermore, NYS

OHCN's focus areas of occupational diseases and cumulative trauma are somewhat narrow in comparison to the whole range of occupational injuries and illnesses.

Integrating Workers' Compensation into the Health Care System

Health care providers noted that workers' compensation policymakers would need to be strategic to improve integration or coordination of care with the rest of the health care system. Workers' compensation represents just 1 percent of U.S. medical spending, so workers' compensation payers have very little leverage to influence care delivery. Claims administrators also agreed that workers' compensation is unlikely to lead changes in health care delivery because it represents such a small part of the overall system.

One suggestion from a health care provider, however, was that a promising starting point for efforts to improve coordination between occupational health care and broader health systems is the prevention of chronic pain and transition to long-term disability. It was asserted that health systems generally lack successful models for preventing musculoskeletal injuries from progressing to chronic pain and that successful quality improvement efforts within the workers' compensation system (such as the COHE model) could make it attractive for employers and health systems to take the steps needed to enable the better coordination of care in other areas of occupational health care. It was pointed out that diagnoses that are widespread in the workers' compensation system (including low back pain, neck pain, and other musculoskeletal disorders) are well represented among the top ten conditions for years lived with a disability in the United States. Other conditions that result in a substantial burden of years lived with a disability in the United States include mental disorders and chronic conditions that are frequently work related but may not always be covered by the workers' compensation system (e.g., major depression, anxiety disorders, and chronic obstructive pulmonary disease [COPD]). This overlap between work-related health conditions and the burden of disability suggests that disability prevention could be a useful focus for workers' compensation policymakers and payers seeking to gain buy-in from health systems for efforts at the improved integration or coordination of care.[4]

One health care provider highlighted the recent merger (finalized in February 2018) of U.S. Health Works and Concentra as an illustration that the trends toward consolidation in the broader U.S. health care market may also be affecting occupational health care delivery. Health care providers viewed the issue of consolidation as poorly understood. The health economics literature finds that hospital consolidation tends to raise prices and may lower quality, but the cost and quality implications of consolidation *within* occupational health care are, to our knowledge, completely unexplored (Gaynor and Town, 2012).

Other useful suggestions for system change strategies were put forward. One health care provider noted that large self-insured employers (including state agencies) or multiemployer

---

[4] Institute for Health Metrics and Evaluation, 2018.

health and welfare trusts for unionized industries could serve as promising platforms for pilot efforts to integrate occupational and nonoccupational care delivery.

The idea of integrated delivery for both workers' compensation and group health care is not new, of course, and a number of subtle barriers to such "24-hour care" efforts have been identified. As single-payer health care has attracted new political attention in some U.S. states, a clearer understanding of the potential consequences for and necessary modifications to workers' compensation laws will be important for state policymakers. A recent issue brief from the California Workers' Compensation Institute reviewed these challenges (Webb, Swedlow, and David, 2016).

While some are superficial issues that could readily be addressed by alert legislators (such as modifying workers' compensation statutes to preserve exclusive remedy even if workers' compensation does not finance care), issues such as preserving employer incentives for safety and determining how to preserve first-dollar coverage for occupational injuries will require more careful consideration. Even conceptually straightforward modifications to coordinate workers' compensation with a single-payer system might require changes to state constitutions, making the political efforts involved far more complex.

Integration of Function and Work Disability Concepts into Health Care Delivery

Colorado is a system that has taken major steps to facilitate and incentivize functional status monitoring by physicians serving workers' compensation patients. A recently initiated program known as Quality Performance and Outcomes Payments (QPOP) may offer a template for the incorporation of functional assessments into health care.[5] The state workers' compensation agency (Colorado Division of Workers' Compensation [DOWC]) developed a list of approved functional tests for a range of physical impairments to various body parts, as well as specific psychological impairments and risk factors. DOWC also modified the state's fee schedule to allow reimbursement for functional assessment for physicians who complete training and obtain a certification from DOWC.

Advances in Health Records and Education Are Needed

Health care providers suggested that NIOSH could play a role in guiding the incorporation of occupation, industry, and functional information into electronic health records. Such information would be beneficial for research and surveillance and, to the extent that this information is important in occupational medicine, the inclusion of this information in electronic health records

---

[5] To our knowledge, the effects of the QPOP initiative on worker outcomes or system costs have not been formally evaluated. A brief overview of the QPOP program for participating providers is available from Pinnacol Assurance, which is Colorado's state fund (Pinnacol Assurance, 2018).

could also improve the coordination of care between workers' compensation and nonoccupational health systems.

Better physician education on disability management, functional improvement, and the rules of the workers' compensation system was also highlighted as a priority by health care providers and workers. Workers felt that physicians in the broader health care system had essentially no training in occupational safety and health, preventing many treating physicians from helping workers engage productively with the workers' compensation system or coordinating with employers. Nonoccupational physicians may also fail to recognize the contribution of working conditions to health problems.

In addition to physician education, it was also suggested that NIOSH and state agencies could have an important role in educating nonphysician adjudicators on the scientific content of treatment guidelines. As noted in Chapter Three, some state agency leaders felt that claims administrators were sometimes too deferential to physician authority and tended to shy away from applying treatment guidelines. While independent appeals mechanisms will always be needed, there was hope that more scientifically fluent claims administrators might be less dependent on cost containment intermediaries, who tend to drive up transaction costs and who may be less likely to have patient-focused incentives.

Evidence Needed to Improve Outcomes and Policymaking

Causation of Occupational Diseases and Nontraumatic Injuries

Several stakeholder groups expressed hope that the development of better data sets for monitoring worker health could lead to a better understanding of causation and work-relatedness for occupational diseases and nontraumatic injuries. Employers, in particular, hoped that better research could point toward best practices for apportionment of disability to nonoccupational cause or that a more robust set of presumptions could be developed to reduce disputes about causation. Similarly, claims administrators felt that the evidence base for occupational disease presumptions was inadequate and that a more definitive and current list of occupational diseases that should be presumptively covered would be a valuable policy contribution.

Some employers felt that workers' contributions to their injuries and illnesses through lifestyle choices should not be the responsibility of the workers' compensation system. Employers also voiced concern that problems with population health—specifically, the prevalence of chronic disease and risk factors, such as obesity—made injury more likely and disability more difficult to manage. The extent to which nonoccupational comorbidities can or should be factored into assessment of causation or apportionment of disability was identified as a place where independent research would be valuable. Meanwhile, stakeholders suggested that understanding how the psychological side effects of an injury can affect the medical and disability outcomes of a claim would also be important; one employer further emphasized the importance of employee engagement in shaping disability and return-to-work outcomes as an area for future research. However, worker advocates pointed out that efforts to apportion disability to occupational and nonoccupational causes tend to undermine the no-fault character of the workers' compensation system by shifting the burden of proof to workers.

A potential role for NIOSH and, perhaps, other federal research sponsors would be the creation of large research data sets combining data on occupational and nonoccupational exposures with information about morbidity. Previous research, most notably the Whitehall studies in Britain, has found persistent associations between work environment, job characteristics, and morbidity for specific conditions (Kuper and Marmot, 2003; Marmot et al., 1991). Ongoing monitoring of these relationships for a broad range of conditions would reduce frictions in contentious areas of workers' compensation decisionmaking, such as the apportionment of causation to workplace factors. Workers suggested that, although some data are extensively analyzed by certain state systems, information about exposures, comorbidities, and disability over the life course is generally not available for large enough populations to study many specific conditions in detail.

Improving Dispute Resolution

Employers expressed considerable interest in alternative dispute resolution and other steps that would make the system easier to navigate for injured workers while reducing the volume of litigation. They were also hopeful that clearer presumptions for the causation of particular conditions could help avoid litigation.

Research on legal arrangements (such as standards of causation or the structure of the medicolegal process) was highlighted by state agency leaders as an area where NIOSH could help to identify best practices. In the absence of rigorous evidence, stakeholders identified several models that might offer a model for reducing disputes and transaction costs in the system in ways that promote return to work without undermining workers' access to compensation and due process.

One of the worker advocates highlighted Washington's program for asbestos workers as an example of a system that had been designed to lower transaction costs and frictions by avoiding reliance on intermediaries. Washington L&I has a program that will presumptively pay lost time benefits to workers with asbestos-related diseases after collecting evidence on their work history and medical conditions. What is notable about this program is that L&I provides worker advocacy services and streamlines the process from the worker's point of view in part to reduce transaction costs; L&I then pursues compensation from employers or insurers.

Employers expressed a range of views about how to address congestion and transaction costs in the workers' compensation system. Carve-outs for specific groups were presented as a promising way to reduce litigation and overall costs, at least in public sector or unionized workplaces. Employers believed that carve-outs led to secondary benefits, such as better labor relations, and suggested that the overall effects of these arrangements deserved more careful study.

Carve-out arrangements, in which employers work with labor unions to integrate occupational and nonoccupational benefits, frequently involve alternative dispute resolution mechanisms. Carve-outs might offer more promise for developing evenhanded alternatives to litigation than the Texas model. The California labor code has provided for carve-outs in all unionized workplaces since 2003 (and in construction since 1993). Nearly 80,000 California employers participated in carve-outs as of 2016. However, since carve-outs are premised on the existence of a union that can serve as the bargaining representative of the workforce, it is unclear how the carve-out model could be generalized to nonunion workplaces. To the extent that fair dispute resolution (for example, the neutrality of ombudsmen, mediators, and arbitrators) is monitored by oversight from both the union and employer sides, it seems unlikely that alternative dispute resolution could be used on a large scale in nonunion workplaces in the absence of far-reaching regulatory efforts by the state agency—in which case efficiency gains relative to litigation would appear less likely. In fact, a state agency leader familiar with carve-outs indicated that carve-outs had not appreciably reduced the volume of litigation, even if they had other such advantages as facilitating integration of occupational and nonoccupational health care. Although state agency leaders identified dispute resolution and excessive litigation as an important obstacle preventing workers' compensation systems from promoting worker well-being, they did not share the optimism of employers about carve-outs or alternative dispute resolution mechanisms as a simple fix.

In principle, the Texas opt-out model could offer one way for employers to develop alternative dispute resolution mechanisms without the regulatory overhead of carve-out programs. Some employers voiced enthusiasm for the Texas model, noting that the strict claim reporting deadlines imposed by many employers' voluntary occupational benefit plans tended to promote early injury reporting and facilitated more effective disability management. However, workers were vehemently opposed to the Texas model of permitting employers to forego workers' compensation and design alternative injury benefit plans without any state standards. The opt-out plans developed in Texas would seem to give some indication of how alternative dispute resolution would look in nonunion workplaces in the absence of minimum standards, and it is clear that the worker advocates who participated in our study viewed these processes—which frequently involve binding arbitration with arbitrators chosen by the employer—as grossly unjust to workers. Without much stronger evidence on how injured workers (including those who do not file injury claims) fare under the opt-out arrangements developed in Texas, it will be difficult to judge whether the Texas model provides net social benefits or, as suggested by workers, simply saves money for employers by reducing workers' access to benefits.

Evidence on Cost Spillovers from Workers' Compensation to Other Insurance Systems

Worker advocates identified the potentially large proportion of health care and disability costs borne outside the workers' compensation system as an important structural reason for underinvestment in prevention and worker health. These costs not only include spillovers from work-related disability to other social insurance programs, such as SSDI and Medicare, but also costs borne by family members and communities of injured workers. Recent research, for example, has found associations between occupational injury and increased health care utilization of family members, possibly driven by increased caregiving needs (Asfaw et al., 2015). Research has also identified an association between workers' compensation claiming and group health insurance claims, suggesting potential cost spillovers from work-related injuries to general health care (Bhattacharya and Park, 2012). Although there is compelling evidence for the causal relationship between workplace injury and subsequent long-term disability, clearer evidence on the extent of these cost spillovers could help motivate policy changes that would help encourage workers' compensation payers and employers to internalize the long-term costs of unsafe working conditions (O'Leary et al., 2012).

Technological Change, Work Arrangements, and Evolving Labor Laws

State agency leaders also highlighted the evolution of employee definitions, potentially including the new classes of worker that could provide alternatives to independent contractor status for the growing population of alternative work arrangements as an area where federal guidance could improve coordination between states and where analysis of the safety and workers' compensation implications of such changes would be welcome.

For workers in certain types of alternative work arrangements, the Right to Know law adopted in Massachusetts was identified by worker advocates as a promising approach to help temporary workers access the workers' compensation system. Under this law, temporary agencies are required to provide workers with a written "job order" that details contact information for the temporary agency, its workers' compensation carrier, and the host employer, as well as the nature of the job to be performed and the work hours and pay. We were not able to find a rigorous evaluation of the extent to which the Right to Know law improved safety or access to benefits for temporary workers. Future research could focus on the effectiveness of the Massachusetts Right to Know law and similar laws in California and Illinois that clarified the sharing of responsibility between agencies and host employers.[6] Worker advocates indicated that right-to-know laws should not be viewed as a panacea, however, and suggested that OSHA or

---

[6] For additional details, see Commonwealth of Massachusetts, undated; Tanenbaum, 2015; and Illinois General Assembly, undated.

state regulators might want to use outreach, education, or enforcement to improve working conditions for workers in alternative work arrangements. The spread of alternative work arrangements seems likely to continue, so these issues are likely to become a larger priority in the future.

Chapter Five. Suggestions for a Research Agenda to Improve Workers' Compensation Policy

Better workers' compensation policy has immense potential to improve worker health, safety, and economic security for all American workers, both through injury prevention and by improving outcomes for workers after injury and illness. Although stakeholders identified many serious problems with currently existing workers' compensation systems, there was no shortage of constructive suggestions for both modest and far-reaching policy changes that seem likely to promote worker well-being.

All stakeholder groups indicated that federal research funders could have a substantial public health consequence by producing independent evidence to inform the ideal design of state workers' compensation systems. Although specific research directions highlighted by stakeholders—such as workers' compensation system design, occupational health care delivery, or disability prevention—might appear to depart from some traditional lines of NIOSH research, the recommended research activities would clearly further the mission of NIOSH as a public health agency focused on OSH. However, health care providers and workers also saw considerable public health value in current NIOSH activities focused on helping states make their workers' compensation data more useful for injury surveillance, for analytics to support prevention and policy evaluation, and for other research. The surveillance and data improvement activities supported through NIOSH's Center for Workers' Compensation Studies, for instance, were highlighted by a health care provider as a promising model for future NIOSH engagement with state workers' compensation systems and public health agencies.

Stakeholders also felt that NIOSH, with its focus on translation of knowledge into practice, should help to communicate these practices to state workers' compensation policymakers. While federal standards for workers' compensation were viewed as politically infeasible or even undesirable by most stakeholder groups other than workers, stakeholders felt that the lack of an evidence base pointing toward the optimal design of a workers' compensation system made it challenging for states to identify independent actions that would improve their own systems. Stakeholders generally agreed that policy evaluation, identification of system best practices, and continued investment in the basic science of epidemiology and applied or translational work on prevention could be valuable activities for NIOSH.

NIOSH is not the only federal research funder that might be able to further its mission by expanding research on workers' compensation policy and occupational health. Federal agencies that bear the brunt of cost spillovers from workers' compensation systems (primarily CMS and SSA) might find it in their interest to invest in research and demonstrations that would leverage the strengths and specialties of existing workers' compensation delivery systems to address the system failures that result in amplified public and private costs following workplace injury.

Meanwhile, federal research agencies might find it beneficial to attend more closely to occupational health and workers' compensation policy as part of their core missions. Agencies and institutes with an explicit focus on disability and aging—such as DOL ODEP, the National Institute on Aging (NIA), and the National Institute on Disability, Independent Living, and Rehabilitation Research (NIDILRR)—would constitute the most obvious research funders for research on workers' compensation, accommodation and employment of people with disabilities, and occupational risk factors for diseases of aging. However, it is also likely such research could be important for a wider range of national institutes focused on diseases with occupational etiologies or where occupational health screenings can play a meaningful role in early detection and disease management. These might include the National Cancer Institute (NCI), the National Heart, Lunch, and Blood Institute (NHLBI), the National Institute of Arthritis and Musculoskeletal and Skin Diseases (NIAMSD), the National Institute on Deafness and Other Communication Disorders (NIDCD), the National Institute of Environmental Health Sciences (NIEHS), or the National Institute on Minority Health and Health Disparities (NIMHD). A list of

Table 5.1: Potential Research Funders and Research Priorities

Type of Organization	Name	Organizational Mission	Research Opportunities
Federal	NIOSH	To develop new knowledge in the field of OSH and to transfer that knowledge into practice	Best practices for workers' compensation systems; occupational disease and injury epidemiology/ surveillance; prevention of workplace hazards; burden of injury/illness; occupational health services research and evaluation of alternative models for occupational health care delivery
	SSA	To promote the economic security of Americans	Cost spillovers and long-term disability prevention
	CMS	To serve beneficiaries of Medicare and Medicaid	Cost spillovers and improving medical delivery/integration with occupational health care; payment reforms to incentivize functional improvement
	DOL ODEP	To develop and influence policies and practices that increase the number and quality of employment opportunities for people with disabilities	Employment of people with disabilities, including stay-at-work/return-to-work efforts

Table 5.1: Potential Research Funders and Research Priorities—Continued

Type of Organization	Name	Organizational Mission	Research Opportunities
Federal	NIA	To support genetic, biological, clinical, behavioral, social, and economic research on aging; foster the development of researchers; provide research resources; and disseminate information to the public	Disability prevention; return-to-work efforts for older workers
	NIDILRR	To maximize the independence, well-being, and health of older adults, people with disabilities across the lifespan, and their families and caregivers	Employment of people with disabilities, including vocational rehabilitation; effects of injury/illness on family members and caregivers; long-term care and home health care delivery
	Other national institutes, including NCI, NHLBI, and NIAMSD	Disease-specific fundamental research; training of medical professionals; and dissemination of information	Occupational and nonoccupational causation of specific diseases and conditions; medical education for disability management
State	State-level workers' compensation agencies	Prevention and management of workplace injuries; information dissemination	Process improvements and demonstration projects; state-specific policy evaluations or analyses to design policy reforms
Private Foundation	Robert Wood Johnson Foundation	To raise the health of Americans and place well-being at the center of every aspect of life	Injury prevention; cost spillovers; process improvements
	Ford Foundation	To reduce poverty and injustice, strengthen democratic values, promote international cooperation, and advance human achievement	Workplace accommodation and vocational rehabilitation; contribution of occupational safety to economic and health inequality
	Regional foundations, including the New York State Health Foundation, the Hogg Foundation for Mental Health, the California Wellness Foundation, and the Colorado Health Foundation	To improve regional health	Demonstration projects; integration of occupational and general health systems; prevention of disability; state-specific studies

potential funders and research opportunities is shown in Table 5.1. We did not evaluate whether the funders listed in Table 5.1 might be subject to legal restrictions on their activities that would prevent them from pursuing these research questions, so our suggestions should be viewed as preliminary. It may be constructive for the federal agencies listed in Table 5.1 to communicate with one another to coordinate their research activities.

Other potential research funders include philanthropic foundations with topic areas related to the social determinants of health or health systems. National research programs (e.g., the Robert Wood Johnson Foundation's Culture of Health initiative) and regional foundations (e.g., the New York State Health Foundation, the Hogg Foundation for Mental Health [in Texas], the California Wellness Foundation, and the Colorado Health Foundation) might see research on occupational health as a bridge between health services research and evaluations of interventions related to socioeconomic outcomes, such as persistent poverty and inequality, which are often linked to experiences in the workplace. Initiatives related to expanding economic opportunity and justice, such as the Ford Foundation's Future of Work program and the Chan Zuckerberg Initiative–funded Opportunity@Work program, might identify research on best practices in return-to-work and disability determination as within the scope of their mission.

Priorities for the National Institute for Occupational Safety and Health and Other Federal Research on Workers' Compensation

One claims administrator summed up the state of research on workers' compensation policy as follows: "[W]e haven't really defined the optimum state or the best workers' comp system that should be available." If NIOSH or other funders chose to pursue research needed to identify the best possible workers' compensation system, a research agenda might proceed along two tracks.

First, state policy experimentation in workers' compensation could be encouraged in part by federal investments and support for rigorous, independent evaluations. NIOSH has pursued such a model through their partnership with Ohio BWC, while such states as Colorado and Washington (sometimes with involvement or research support from NIOSH and other federal agencies) have pursued extensive experimentation largely on their own initiative. A promising effort in this vein is currently being developed by DOL ODEP in partnership with SSA, which will sponsor up to eight state pilot programs intended to test stay-at-work/return-to-work interventions for various disabled populations, likely including workers' compensation claimants.[1] A key component of the Retaining Employment and Talent After Injury/Illness (RETAIN) Demonstration Projects (as this effort is known) will be an independent evaluation. As suggested by our stakeholder participants, injury prevention, occupational health care

---

[1] DOL ODEP, 2018.

delivery, and disability management would appear to be promising areas for more experimental efforts, potentially including medical payment reform or quality improvement and coordination of care efforts similar to COHE or NYS OHCN.

Second, in addition to the evaluation of innovative policy interventions, stakeholders also identified a need for a wide range of more basic scientific, economic, and other social-scientific evidence on questions pertaining to epidemiology, system performance, and financing. Many important questions, particularly those related to causation, apportionment, and occupational disease presumptions, will generally require observational study and epidemiological methods.

To maximize policy impact, these efforts should be guided wherever possible by explicit theories of employment outcomes, disability progression, employer decisionmaking, and other relevant behaviors. Similarly, policy development should be informed, when possible, by conceptual frameworks that enable quantitative tradeoffs between competing social objectives. By specifying mechanisms through which interventions and systems affect individual outcomes, such theories will be crucial to help identify precisely what quantities and causal relationships should be identified to most directly inform policy improvement.

Theories about causal mechanisms will also be critical to determining generalizability. There is much to be gained from an experimentalist turn in research on occupational health and disability, and the expansion of large-scale field experiments, such as the RETAIN Demonstration Projects, suggests that the field of disability policy is already moving in this direction. However, experimental evidence and context-specific best practices are unlikely to be enough on their own. Even after successful practices have been designed, implemented, and evaluated in specific settings, questions about external validity for other settings will remain. Theoretical frameworks will be needed to help guide whether policies should be adopted in new environments. The field of development economics, where randomized controlled trials (RCTs) have been far more widespread than in disability policy and OSH, offers some instructive parallels. The experimentalist turn in development economics has produced numerous findings with strong internal validity (Banerjee and Duflo, 2009). Yet problems of generalizability and development of policy implications cannot be addressed without an understanding of theoretical mechanisms. The economist Angus Deaton put it as follows: "RCTs of 'what works,' even when done without error or contamination, are unlikely to be helpful for policy, or to move beyond the local, unless they tell us something about why the program worked, something to which they are often neither targeted nor well-suited" (Deaton, 2010). Stakeholder insights discussed above into why the COHE model might not generalize to Montana give a good example of the problems that await OSH researchers and workers' compensation policymakers once more success stories have been successfully demonstrated. Given the complexity of workers' compensation systems and their historically independent development across state lines, it is not hard to imagine debate about whether successful system designs from Washington will generalize to Texas becoming as contentious as arguments about whether an education program from urban India will work in rural Brazil.

43

Economic theory, fortunately, provides numerous frameworks for optimal policy design that would appear to be directly applicable to many of the challenges facing workers' compensation. One research approach might combine modeling frameworks from the public finance literature on optimal social insurance with more rigorous evidence on factors affecting return to work and the accuracy of existing disability rating approaches to provide a theoretical foundation for redesigning disability rating and benefit schedules. For example, Hunt and Dillender (2017), interpreting findings from Savych and Hunt (2017), note that Michigan's wage loss approach to disability compensation (in conjunction with other unique system features) leads to much better benefit adequacy than has been found in states that use permanent disability ratings to assign benefits. The argument against a wage loss approach is that it discourages return to work by creating a high implicit tax rate on labor earnings, whereas rating-based systems decouple workers' disability benefits from their work outcomes (Reville et al., 2005). Economic theory tells us that the choice between these two approaches fundamentally involves a tradeoff between the social benefit of more adequate benefits and the social cost of distortions in workers' labor supply decisions, both quantities that can and should be measured empirically (Chetty and Finkelstein, 2013). Similarly, more complete evidence on the epidemiology of occupational disease or other chronic conditions could be used to guide the development of optimal presumptions or apportionment rules within the context of a formal model of health over the life cycle accounting for potentially endogenous investments in health care and preventative behaviors (Grossman, 1972; Ravesteijn, Van Kippersluis, and Van Doorslaer, 2018).

Theories of value-based payment, value-based insurance design, and optimal insurance when agents are systematically irrational (i.e., behavioral public finance) can be combined with evidence on the behavior of patients, health care providers, and employers to design more effective health care payments and incentives to provide accommodation (Chernew, Rosen, and Fendrick, 2010; Robinson, 2001; Baicker, Mullainathan, and Schwartzstein, 2015). Furthermore, explicit theorizing about optimal policy design holds the promise to produce insights into which policies are best under different circumstances. Rather than recommending a single model workers' compensation system for states that differ widely on important dimensions, such as health care rate-setting, industry mix, labor law, or unionization rates, social science theory should be able to help policymakers understand the inherent tradeoffs and contextual factors that will determine which workers' compensation policies will be best for workers in their state.

Finally, we note that the research priorities highlighted in this report were, to some extent, circumscribed by stakeholders' perceptions of political feasibility and an interest in building incrementally on existing workers' compensation systems. In general, the range of policy experimentation and research questions suggested here largely consists of changes around the margins of existing workers' compensation systems, such as reforming care delivery and case management, promoting injury prevention, or developing active labor market programs to promote return to work. The incrementalist outlook held by our stakeholder participants reflects favorably on the durability of the grand bargain: stakeholders generally appeared to be interested in preserving the key elements of workers' compensation.

There is also, however, a need for research that periodically reevaluates the appropriateness of this basic structure, given that the economy, the health care system, and social policy have evolved dramatically in the century since the first workers' compensation systems were adopted in the United States. For instance, Frank Neuhauser has suggested that workers in low- and medium-risk occupations—which he defines to include 90 percent of workers—would be better off if workers' compensation disability benefits were replaced with a universal all-cause disability insurance program and if medical care for injured workers were simply delivered by universal health insurance coverage (Neuhauser, 2016). Given that some states are actively exploring the development of single-payer health care delivery systems, there could soon be a need for detailed analysis of what role workers' compensation should play in financing and care delivery in the context of a single-payer system. Stakeholder discussion of integrating workers' compensation medical care with the broader health care system generally presupposed a distinction between workers' compensation and other health care payers, but one could imagine more radical forms of coordination with group health, such as replacing workers' compensation medical benefits with capitated payments to group health plans (a model referred to as "24-hour care" in the 1990s). Although a pilot experiment with such arrangements in California was abandoned after relatively low take-up, implementation of universal health insurance coverage would create new opportunities to revisit the relationship between workers' compensation and other health care delivery systems. As noted above, carve-out arrangements and other delivery models might offer some lessons to inform more ambitious reforms.

Certain policy challenges that might be amenable to fundamental reforms or entirely new insurance arrangements should also be an occasion for policy analysts to develop more detailed policy proposals. The narrowing coverage of occupational diseases and conditions with complex causation or high latency might create a need for compensation mechanisms to be financed and operated outside state workers' compensation systems, perhaps on the model of the federal programs for specific diseases and populations, such as black lung disease or 9/11 first responders. Meanwhile, if alternative work arrangements continue to become more prevalent without the expansion of workers' compensation systems to cover these workers, new forms of disability insurance and health care financing might become necessary. The development of insurance mechanisms for workers and conditions that are currently excluded from the workers' compensation system could provide a useful laboratory for financing and delivery models that might help strengthen existing compensation systems.

To sum up, there is much that NIOSH and other research sponsors could do to produce rigorous evidence on the design of an optimal workers' compensation system without disturbing the basic structure of workers' compensation or revisiting the normative principles endorsed in the 1972 national commission report. Stakeholders expressed pessimism about the likelihood that workers and employers would reach the same degree of consensus today about the objectives of workers' compensation policy.

Regardless of stakeholders' particular economic interests, however, the policy evaluation and epidemiological and theoretical work needed to guide optimal policy development should be recognized as contributing to system efficiency and social welfare. The major themes that emerged from our discussions—including improvements in health care delivery, better integration with nonoccupational health care, injury prevention, improved system navigation, and disability prevention—are all areas where buy-in from both workers and employers is likely because all these goals have the potential to achieve cost savings by promoting better worker outcomes. NIOSH and other research funders could do much to improve the performance of workers' compensation systems.

Appendix A: Discussion Participants

Table A.1: Stakeholder Group Discussion Participants

Stakeholder Group	Name	Affiliation
Workers and Workers' Advocates	Brian Sherlock	Transport Workers Union of America (AFL-CIO)
	Debbie Berkowitz	National Employment Law Project (NELP)
	Mark Catlin	Service Employees International Union (SEIU)
	David DeSario	Alliance for the American Temporary Workforce
	Andy Comai	United Auto Workers
State Agencies	Victoria Kennedy	Washington L&I
	Christine Baker	California Department of Industrial Relations
	Mark Long	Michigan Workers' Compensation Agency
	Elizabeth Crum	Pennsylvania Department of Labor and Industry
	Lou Savage	Oregon Workers' Compensation Division
	Bill Wheeler	Montana Department of Labor and Industry
Health Care	Gary Franklin	Washington L&I
	Linda Forst	University of Illinois at Chicago School of Public Health
	Peter Orris	University of Illinois at Chicago Medical Center
	Margaret Cook-Shimanek	Resources for Environmental and Occupational Health (Montana)
	Bob Harrison	California Department of Public Health
	Kathryn Mueller	DOWC (Colorado)
Claims Administrators/Insurers	Dave Bonauto	Washington L&I
	Bridgette Matthews	SAIF Corporation
	Alex Swedlow	California Workers' Compensation Institute
	Abe Tarawneh	Ohio BWC
	Carl Heinlein	American Contractors Insurance Group; American Industrial Hygiene Association
Employers	Peggy Sugarman	City and County of San Francisco
	Barbara Dawson	DuPont
	Doug Holmes	UWC Strategic Services on Unemployment and Workers' Compensation
	Michael Trusty	Walmart

Appendix B: Overview of Workers' Compensation Systems

This appendix provides background information on workers' compensation systems in the United States. The overview draws heavily on Utterback, Meyers, and Wurzelbacher (2014), which provides a more detailed introduction to workers' compensation policy for readers with a public health background. We recommend that readers seeking additional information consult that report and references therein. This document also contains a thorough glossary of workers' compensation terminology that may be useful to readers who are less familiar with workers' compensation policy.

Overview of Workers' Compensation Systems

Workers' compensation is a state-level social insurance program that provides financial, medical, and rehabilitation benefits to workers who sustain job-related injuries or illnesses. Workers' compensation systems are characterized by a "grand bargain" between employers and employees—in exchange for access to no-fault benefits, employees accept the workers' compensation system as an exclusive remedy for workplace injuries, foregoing their rights to pursue tort claims against their employers. In general, covered employers are required to finance workers' compensation benefits through premiums paid to a workers' compensation insurer or through self-insurance. Premium costs typically relate to the injury risk at a workplace in two ways: actuarial risk classifications, which are based on industry, the size of the firm, and the mix of employees at a worksite; and experience modification factors, which adjust premiums up or down according to a workplace's claims history relative to its classification (Utterback, Meyers, and Wurzelbacher, 2014). The combination of no-fault disability benefits and medical care, exclusive remedy protection from tort liability, provision of vocational rehabilitation services, and workplace safety incentives, such as experience-rating, forms the basis of most workers' compensation systems.

In 2015, an estimated 136 million workers in the United States were covered by workers' compensation, accounting for approximately 97 percent of jobs covered by unemployment insurance and 86 percent of all jobs (McLaren and Baldwin, 2017). Since the inception of workers' compensation programs in the early twentieth century, coverage and benefits have varied widely across states. Grounds for exemption of certain employers include firm size, industry, job tenure, and employee classification (i.e., sole proprietor, independent contractor, family member, self-employed, etc.). Agricultural employees are excluded from coverage in some states, and some states have special carve-outs for such high-risk industries as mining and construction (Utterback, Meyers, and Wurzelbacher, 2014). Minimum employee thresholds for compulsory workers' compensation coverage range from one to five across most states. State workers' compensation systems also differ in the generosity of benefits, the injuries and diseases that are covered (including presumptions for specified disease-industry pairs), the procedures for determining the extent to which an injury or disease is work related, rules regulating the provision of medical benefits (such as limits on physician choice, fee schedules, and time to file claims), and resources available for vocational rehabilitation.

States have developed distinct approaches to administering and regulating workers' compensation systems. All states have a workers' compensation agency, whose core responsibilities are processing workers' compensation claims, facilitating dispute resolution, tracking worker outcomes, informing stakeholders of their roles, rights, and responsibilities in the workers' compensation system, and implementing state-level policy reforms related to workers' compensation (Utterback, Meyers, and Wurzelbacher, 2014). Insurance markets also vary considerably across states. Currently, four states (Ohio, North Dakota, Washington, and Wyoming) operate exclusive state insurance funds, meaning all covered employers in those states must purchase their workers' compensation coverage from the state insurer or self-insure. Twenty-two states operate state funds that compete with private insurers, while the remainder are exclusively private (Szymendera, 2017). One state, Texas, has required employers to opt into the workers' compensation system since the system was created in 1913 and still does today. Texas employers who do not opt into workers' compensation forego protection from litigation for work-related injuries, and employees at those firms are not eligible for indemnity, medical, or vocational rehabilitation benefits associated with workers' compensation.

Types of Benefits

Workers' compensation insurance benefits can cover lost earnings, medical treatment, vocational rehabilitation, and costs related to permanent disability and death (Utterback, Meyers, and Wurzelbacher, 2014). State laws regulating these benefits vary considerably across states, but some features are consistent across all workers' compensation systems: cash payments for lost earnings are tax-free, medical services are provided at no cost to the injured worker, and workers' compensation claimants can retroactively recoup unpaid benefits for the time between the onset of their injury and when they become eligible for benefits, known as the waiting period. While waiting periods and levels of benefits vary by state, an important feature shared by all states is that workers' compensation benefits are subject to statutory maximums and are generally limited to partial compensation for economic losses (i.e., loss of actual earnings or earnings capacity). Combined with the exclusive remedy doctrine, the definition of workers' compensation benefits in terms of economic losses prevents workers from recovering important categories of damages that are recoverable in tort, including loss of function unrelated to work disability or pain and suffering.

Indemnity Benefits

All workers' compensation systems pay tax-free cash, or indemnity, benefits to compensate employees and their families for lost earnings due to work-related injury, illness, and death. Indemnity benefits had historically accounted for the majority of all paid benefits. Medical spending has grown steadily as a share of benefits over time, however, and workers' compensation benefits have been evenly divided between indemnity and medical spending since 2010 (McLaren and Baldwin, 2017). In contrast, the approximately $30.7 billion in indemnities paid in 2015 accounted for slightly less than half of all workers' compensation benefits. In 2013, less than a quarter of all workers' compensation claims involved indemnities.

Indemnity benefits are grouped into two large categories: temporary and permanent. Temporary benefits are paid while the injured worker is recovering from injury, with the duration and level of benefits depending on when—and how fully—the worker is able to return to work. If the injured employee is unable to work in any capacity during this recovery period, the worker will be eligible for *temporary total disability* (TTD) payments, which are designed to compensate for time away from work. In some but not all states, the injured worker will be eligible for *temporary partial disability* (TPD) payments if the worker can return to work in a limited capacity. In some states, the duration of temporary benefits is capped at a specific number of weeks (Utterback, Meyers, and Wurzelbacher, 2014).

Depending on the state's workers' compensation statute, temporary indemnity benefits are reassessed when an injured worker has reached maximum medical improvement (MMI), a determination made by a treating or evaluating physician. At this point, if the injured worker exhibits residual impairment or remains off work (depending on the state), the worker may be eligible for permanent disability payments. If the injury prevents the claimant from performing any kind of work, he or she will be eligible for *permanent total disability* (PTD) benefits. If the claimant can perform some work tasks but is unlikely to improve over time, he or she will be eligible for *permanent partial disability* (PPD) benefits. Permanent disability benefits are paid until the worker reaches retirement age, begins receiving other income support, or for the remainder of the worker's life, depending on state laws. In some cases, time limits for receiving benefits related to specific permanent disabilities, such as the loss of a limb, are written into the state workers' compensation statue.

Benefit amounts in each of these four categories vary with the worker's preinjury earnings, the nature of the injury, and the rules and regulations in the worker's state of employment. A common but not universal benchmark is that benefits should compensate injured workers for two-thirds of their preinjury earnings (McLaren and Baldwin, 2017). States have developed a wide range of different approaches to determining permanent disability benefits; see Appendix A of Reville et al. (2005) for a thorough taxonomy of approaches to disability benefit determination. Today, many states have adopted an impairment-based approach, in which benefits are calculated based on evaluations of impairment conducted according to the American Medical Association's *Guide to the Evaluation of Permanent Impairment* or some other methodology (Utterback, Meyers, and Wurzelbacher, 2014). In all states, benefits are subject to minimums and maximums depending on average wages in the state and laws regulating specific injuries.

In practice, lump-sum settlement agreements between workers, employers, and carriers have increasingly replaced PPD benefits in some states. These settlements release the employer and carrier from obligations to pay future benefits and in some cases may limit the employee's rights to return to work at the at-injury employer (Spieler, 2017). The nature of settlement agreements varies across states and injury types—most but not all states allow settlements that fully resolve a workers' compensation claim regardless of the severity of the injury. In some cases, settlements will only cover indemnities, while others may involve medical coverage as well. State statutes often require state workers' compensation agencies to approve settlement agreements (Utterback, Meyers, and Wurzelbacher, 2014).

Interaction with Other Social Programs

Injured workers can simultaneously receive workers' compensation benefits and SSDI, but combined workers' compensation and SSDI payments cannot exceed 80 percent of preinjury earnings (Szymendera, 2017). Rules for how workers' compensation and SSDI benefits are adjusted to meet this standard vary by state. Workers' compensation also interacts with Medicare as a second payer for work-related health care expenses. Some workers' compensation settlement agreements include Medicare set-asides, in which a portion of the settlement is allocated to future medical expenses, and Medicare will only begin covering medical costs when that allocation has been depleted (CMS, 2018).

Medical Benefits

Workers' compensation insurers are responsible for providing medical treatment for workplace injuries and diseases at no cost to the injured worker. In 2015, medical benefits cost workers' compensation insurers approximately $31.1 billion, a 1 percent increase from 2011 (McLaren and Baldwin, 2017). Medical costs have increased steadily as a percentage of all workers' compensation costs, accounting for more than half of benefit costs in 2015. Most workers' compensation claims involve only medical treatment: in 2013, roughly 75 percent of workers' compensation claims were medical-only, compared to 78 percent in 1995.

Workers' compensation medical services exist alongside but somewhat separate from the general health care system, and other health insurers are typically not authorized to cover work-related medical services (Szymendera, 2017). Accordingly, the provision of medical care in the workers' compensation system is governed by rules and regulations specific to each state. In most cases, these rules are oriented toward controlling costs, given the lack of patient-side cost-sharing in the system. One cost-control measure common to many workers' compensation systems is the use of medical fee schedules, which specify reimbursement rates for workers' compensation–related health services (Utterback, Meyers, and Wurzelbacher, 2014). Other policy instruments that vary widely across states include time limits for filing claims (and therefore initiating medical benefits); limits on physician choice, such as whether the worker or insurer can choose their doctor and whether only approved doctors can treat workers' compensation claimants; restrictions on utilization of medical services, such as office visits; and guidelines for utilization review, the process for determining whether medical treatments covered by workers' compensation insurance are medically necessary.

Vocational Rehabilitation

Workers' compensation systems require insurers to provide eligible workers with vocational rehabilitation services designed to improve their ability to return to work, either in their preinjury role, a different role at the same employer, or a new job at a different employer. Vocational rehabilitation services, which are typically voluntary (Szymendera, 2017), may include facilitating communications between employees and their previous employers to identify work opportunities and discuss workplace accommodations; physical rehabilitation; access to education and training, including general job-search training, such as a skills evaluation, resume building, or career counseling; and coordination between injured workers and other stakeholders, including potential employers and the health care system. Vocational rehabilitation services are generally facilitated by the insurance carrier and the state vocational rehabilitation agency.

Workers' compensation benefits are typically designed to incentivize injured workers to return to their job, if possible—workers' compensation claimants receive only a fraction of their preinjury earnings through the workers' compensation system and are therefore financially better off working if they are able. In cases where a medical evaluation concludes the claimant should be able to return to work, the worker will typically be required to do so. In cases where disability removes a worker from a job for an extended period of time, employers are generally not required to hold the job, but specific cases may be regulated by the Family Medical Leave Act (FMLA), the Americans with Disabilities Act (ADA), or state antidiscrimination laws (Szymendera, 2017).

Safety Incentives/Loss Prevention

In addition to providing benefits to injured workers, the encouragement of safety is a key objective of workers' compensation systems (National Commission on State Workmen's Compensation Laws, 1972). In 2015, approximately 2.9 million recordable, nonfatal occupational injuries and diseases were reported in private-sector firms, and 4,836 fatal work-related injuries occurred in all workplaces (McLaren and Baldwin, 2017). Overall injury and disease rates have declined steadily in recent years, but the mix of injuries has changed slightly: the incidence of injuries and illnesses resulting in time away from work declined from 3.6 percent in 1980 to less than 1 percent in 2015; meanwhile, the incidence of cases resulting in job restrictions or job transfer rose in the same period from 0.3 percent to 0.7 percent (McLaren and Baldwin, 2017).[1] It is important to acknowledge, however, that both official injury-rate estimates published by the BLS and counts of workers' compensation claims underestimate the true number of workplace injuries due to underreporting, and it is difficult to infer trends in actual workplace safety from trends in reported injury rates without accounting for potential changes in reporting behavior (McLaren and Baldwin, 2017).

Workers' compensation systems are designed to promote workplace safety through two channels: premium costs and loss prevention services. In general, workers' compensation premiums are determined by a manual, or base rate, and an experience modification factor. The base rate is determined by actuarial average risk across all firms with similar characteristics, such as industry, firm size, and employee mix, and is often set by a third-party actuarial organization or rating bureau (Utterback, Meyers, and Wurzelbacher, 2014). Experience modification factors are determined by the firm's historical injury record relative to its industry risk classification. Experience modification rates tend to be driven more by the frequency of claims than the overall cost of claims, reflecting the goal of reducing the overall rate of workplace injuries. Some observers, however, have said experience-rating incentivizes employers to use aggressive claims management practices that may suppress legitimate claims (Morantz et al., 2016).

Loss prevention programs are another channel through which insurers can promote workplace safety. Through these programs, carriers can assess the injury and illness risks at a worksite and make recommendations or provide inducements to the employer to implement modifications to reduce those risks. The scope of these programs varies, from such low-cost approaches as brochures and safety pamphlets to site visits and inspections (Utterback, Meyers, and Wurzelbacher, 2014). More involved loss prevention practices tend to be targeted at large employers with higher risk of workplace injury; in general, firms who pay higher premiums are more likely to receive loss prevention services.

Financing and Delivery

Workers' compensation systems are almost exclusively funded through premiums paid by employers, though some states also require employee contributions. In 2015, the workers' compensation system cost employers approximately $1.32 per $100 of covered wages and paid out $0.86 per $100 in benefits (McLaren and Baldwin, 2017). System costs have oscillated between a high of $2.18 (in 1990) and a low of $1.27 (in 2010) per $100 of covered wages since 1980, when comparable metrics were first introduced.

Workers' compensation policies available to employers vary widely across states and employer types, and the complexity of policies tends to rise with the complexity of the

---

[1] Readers should take caution in interpreting these differences due to changes in OSHA reporting requirements in 2002 (see McLaren and Baldwin, 2017, p. 48).

workplace. Single-location employers can buy coverage for injuries that occur only at that worksite, while larger employers may purchase policies that span several locations or even account for employee travel across states (Utterback, Meyers, and Wurzelbacher, 2014). Policies also vary by the amount of postinjury risk the employer bears. Some policies, known as guaranteed cost policies, fully insure the employer against the cost of claims. In contrast, employers with high-deductible policies are effectively self-insured up to the deductible, beyond which they are fully insured. Finally, firms can self-insure and face the full cost of their workers' compensation claims. It is worth noting that full self-insurance can be viewed as a form of perfect experience modification: the cost of workers' compensation coverage is proportional to the product of injury rates and average costs. Firms that self-insure may be protected from some systemwide shocks (such as the insurance underwriting cycle) that may raise average premiums above average insurer losses. Eligibility for self-insurance varies by state but is typically only available to large firms. In 2015, among states where self-insurance is possible, the percentage of all benefits paid by self-insured firms ranged from 3.1 percent in Idaho to 52 percent in Alabama (McLaren and Baldwin, 2017).

Given the near-universal nature of workers' compensation coverage in states other than Texas, states have had to develop policies to guarantee the availability of coverage for all covered employers. In states with state funds, the state fund serves as a market of last resort (if not the entire market, as in Ohio, North Dakota, Washington, and Wyoming). In states without state funds, the market of last resort is typically an assigned risk pool. Employers may fail to qualify for coverage in the voluntary market for several reasons, including an insufficient workers' compensation record (i.e., young firms), a record of very high or abnormal claims, or participation in a high-risk industry.

Many states also offer second-injury funds that provide coverage for workplace injuries that interact with preexisting conditions. One motivation for operating second-injury funds is that employers may be reluctant to hire workers with preexisting conditions if they fear the workers are at elevated risk of injury. Twenty states have abolished their second-injury funds since World War II, and others have limited the coverage those funds provide (Szymendera, 2017).

Federal Programs

Though primarily a state system, some of the earliest workers' compensation policies in the United States exclusively covered members of the federal workforce, including an 1882 law covering lost salaries for members of the U.S. Life Saving Service—a life-boat agency—and a 1908 law covering a wider range of risky federal occupations (Szymendera, 2017). Today, all civilian federal employees are covered by the Federal Employees' Compensation Act (FECA), which is similar to most state-based workers' compensation systems and is administered by DOL and financed by the employee's home agency. Several categories of workers whose place of employment is primarily under federal jurisdiction, such as maritime workers, employees of the

District of Columbia, and some civilian staff of the armed services, are covered by the Longshore and Harbor Workers' Compensation Act (LHWCA), which is administered by DOL. More limited workers' compensation programs administered by DOL include benefits for coal miners diagnosed with black lung disease and employees involved in hazardous energy occupations, such as the development and testing of nuclear weapons.

Appendix C: Compendium of Critical Perspectives on Current Workers' Compensation Policy

Background

NIOSH has requested support from RAND to develop, with stakeholder input, a characterization of the most important possible ways to improve workers' compensation systems to promote OSH and worker well-being. To identify current system strengths and policy challenges, RAND will elicit input from a diverse range of stakeholders and experts via a series of small conference calls to be convened in the fall of 2017.

RAND has reviewed recently published critiques of contemporary workers' compensation policy and compiled concerns that have been raised about workers' compensation system performance. This memo is intended to identify a broad range of perspectives on the appropriate goals of workers' compensation policy with respect to OSH and worker outcomes, as well as any notable successes and failure points.

In addition to identifying policy challenges, NIOSH and RAND are interested in obtaining stakeholder perspectives about the most promising options for improving the workers' compensation systems' ability to promote OSH and worker outcomes. This might involve identifying states, insurers, employers, or policy approaches that are succeeding and considering how to generalize these successes to other settings. Institutional, statutory, and other barriers that prevent adoption of proven solutions are also of particular interest. Such barriers might include cases where a solution that would benefit one stakeholder group engenders opposition from another stakeholder group. This project also seeks to identify solutions that appear promising but that currently lack an adequate evidence base.

The strengths and challenges listed below reflect those identified by one or more of the critical pieces we reviewed on the current performance of workers' compensation. Although our primary focus is on issues that affect OSH and worker outcomes, we also include strengths and weaknesses that either have an indirect effect on workers or that reflect important elements of the institutional context for system features that directly affect worker outcomes. Where possible, we have also listed specific suggestions for improvement made by the sources included in our review.

At the end of the project, we hope to have identified a set of constructive suggestions to improve workers' compensation systems over the next five years, as well as insight into what important gaps in knowledge or conflicts between stakeholder interests might pose barriers to adoption of solutions. It will also be valuable to know which directions for system change stakeholders view as most promising.

Goals of Contemporary Workers' Compensation Systems

The major goals identified by the 1972 national commission were

1. broad coverage of employees and work-related injuries and diseases
2. substantial protection against interruption of income
3. provision of sufficient medical care and rehabilitation services
4. encouragement of safety.

A fifth goal that might be viewed as instrumental to promotion of these four goals was also articulated:

5. an effective system for delivery of the benefits and services.

In addition to these worker-oriented goals, the grand bargain of the workers' compensation system is also designed to protect employers from uncertainty and large losses related to workplace injuries at a reasonable and predictable cost in the form of workers' compensation premiums (McLaren and Baldwin, 2016, p. 5). The system also seeks to promote safety in the workplace by creating an institutional environment in which employer efforts to reduce injuries result in lower costs.

In a recent series of "National Conversations," participants at three IAIABC meetings in 2016 were polled about the proper objectives of workers' compensation systems. This group consisted mostly of state and provincial regulators, attorneys and judges, and insurers and other claims administrators; employers and workers were underrepresented. Goals endorsed by a strong majority (over 85 percent of each meeting) included

- a focus on outcomes, including medical recovery and return to work
- a system that reduces complexity
- encouraging safety
- providing equitable benefits to employees at a reasonable cost to employers
- a system that reduces disputes and is less adversarial
- broad coverage for covered employees
- adequate communication to all workers and employers about their rights and responsibilities.

Support was strong but less unanimous across meetings for the propositions that

- workers' compensation should remain the exclusive remedy
- states should define a more uniform mechanism for calculating and paying permanent partial disability.

Support for the following propositions was weaker, with a majority of participants disagreeing in at least one meeting:

- The system should be flexible and adaptable. (One example of successful flexibility cited in the IAIABC conversations is the Texas fee schedule, which is stable but not static. In general, flexibility was seen to be in tension with the stability and predictability of the system.)

- Workers' compensation should be more consistent across U.S. jurisdictions
- The system should cover all working people.

In a recent article providing a sweeping history and evaluation of workers' compensation, Emily Spieler described three "inconsistent narratives" about the purpose of workers' compensation and noted that conflict between stakeholders often reflected clashes between these views of the system:

- workers' compensation as social insurance
- workers' compensation as a no-fault strict liability system
- workers' compensation as a disability management system (Spieler, 2016, p. 89).

This may be a useful framework for understanding the diversity of viewpoints about current system performance.

Overview of Key Workers' Compensation Policy Issues

Workers' Compensation Strengths

- **Workers' compensation has made a strong contribution to economic growth and has promoted workplace safety and stability** (IAIABC, 2016a, p. 3).
- **The workers' compensation system is financially solvent now and into the future**. Workers' compensation in most states is provided through competitive insurance markets where, with few exceptions, premiums are set at levels that support payment of claims without systemwide solvency concerns. Workers' compensation pays reasonable benefits at reasonable rates. In several states, litigation rates on claims are low (less than 10 percent) according to the IAIABC participants (IAIABC, 2016a, p.3; 2016b, p. 3).
- **Coverage is provided to most employees**, with about 97 percent of unemployment insurance–covered employees covered by workers' compensation according to the National Academy of Social Insurance (NASI) estimates for 2014 (McLaren and Baldwin, 2016, p. 16).
- **Injury rates and average injury severity have declined over the last several decades**. According to estimates from BLS, for example, 12 workers are killed on the job each day today compared to approximately 38 in 1970 (OSHA, 2015, p. 12).
  - Beginning in the 1990s, a **culture of safety** emerged in many workplaces, promoting such practices as fall restraints and the use of helmets (Malooly, 2010, p. 45; Spieler, 2016, p. 61).
  - State workers' compensation systems are more cognizant of **occupational diseases** and how to compensate for them (Barth, 2010, p. 14).
- **Insurer-based prevention programs have demonstrated some success in reducing injuries**. Several insurers offer financial incentives for employers to introduce engineering controls and other injury prevention mechanisms. For example, the Ohio

BWC, a state-run insurer, provides matching funds for employers to implement engineering controls, a program that was shown to reduce workers' compensation claim frequency rates by 66 percent (Wurzelbacher, 2017, p. 8).

- **Stakeholders have begun to take advantage of the rich data in the system, and claims administration has become more efficient over time**. There is more automation and less paperwork, and such mechanisms as fee schedules have decreased disagreement and friction in the system. The use of tools, such as the autocoding of data fields, has improved the validity of claims data (Wurzelbacher, 2017, p. 7).
- **Widespread commitment to the grand bargain is voiced by stakeholders within the system** (i.e., regulators, insurers, and employers and unions who participate in IAIABC conversations) (IAIABC, 2016b, p. 2).
- **Some state programs have demonstrated success in facilitating return to work**. Two programs from Washington State, for example, have been shown to be effective. The COHE program, which fosters communication between stakeholders during the return-to-work process, has been shown to reduce disability days, labor force exits, total workers' compensation costs, and entry to SSDI (Stapleton and Christian, 2016, p. 10). Washington state's Stay at Work Program provides financial incentives for employers who return their injured workers to employment and boasts a return on investment of $2.40 for every $1.00 in reimbursement costs, driven by avoided time-loss payments and anticipated reductions in long-term disability payments (IAIABC Disability Management and Return to Work Committee, 2016, p. 46). In addition, activity coaching programs have been shown to facilitate return to work, whether at the original employer or not.
- More doctors and claim administrators are embracing the biopsychosocial model, understanding return to work is influenced by more than a workplace injury (Horejsh, 2017; IAIABC, 2016a, p. 3).

Workers' Compensation Challenges

System Administration

- **The system is too complex**, and variability in benefits, reporting requirements, forms, employee definitions, dispute processes, and other design features across jurisdictions creates confusion about what is compensable.
  - **There is too much emphasis on compliance, not outcomes**: reforms have led to increased compliance burdens (reporting, forms, etc.) for employers and claims administrators. Compliance is often perceived as unrelated to promoting good outcomes (IAIABC, 2016a, p. 2).
  - News reports by ProPublica have highlighted the **disparity in outcomes resulting from variation in benefit rates across jurisdictions** (Grabell and Berkes, 2015a).
  - **Increased complexity in the general health care system** has trickled into workers' compensation, increasing overall administrative costs and the complexity of the system (Mueller and Harris, 2010, p. 152).
  - **Payor systems have become more complex** (IAIABC, 2016b, p. 5).

- **Dispute resolution can be slow, difficult to navigate, and unfair to workers.** Some may settle away substantive or procedural rights to obtain timely medical care or income (DOL, 2016, pp. 21–22; Barth, 2010, p. 16; IAIABC, 2016b, p. 5).
- Policy innovations, such as **fee restrictions for claimants' lawyers**, have decreased employees' ability to navigate an increasingly complex system (DOL, 2016, p. 17; Burton, 2016, p. 4).

- **Limited resources for system regulators** prevent most states from playing an active role in helping workers navigate the system.

  - **Agencies have difficulty filling jobs and competing with private-sector salaries** for specialized skill sets/deep institutional knowledge needed to manage workers' compensation (IAIABC, 2016d, p. 4; Crum, 2010, p. 194).

Suggestions for Improvement

- Look for opportunities to increase uniformity across jurisdictions, starting with waiting periods, proof-of-coverage requirements, minimum benefits and caps, notice posters, adoption of current protocol terminology (CPT) coding methodology, consistency in medical billing processes, and adoption of formularies and treatment guidelines (IAIABC, 2016b, p. 6).
- Increase use of alternative dispute resolution and mediation mechanisms (IAIABC, 2016b, p. 5).
- Remove unnecessary regulations, administrative processes, and forms. Legislation is not necessarily needed to resolve extreme cases (e.g., the top 1 percent of claims) (IAIABC, 2016c, p. 6).
- Incentivize efficient administration by introducing sunset provisions, as in Texas (IAIABC, 2016b, p. 5).
- Allow for options other than hard copy checks to pay indemnity benefits. Also, eliminate "dual" administrative processes: paper and electronic data interchange (EDI) (IAIABC, 2016c).
- Properly fund state workers' compensation agencies, and ensure wages are competitive with industry (IAIABC, 2016b, p. 5).

Coverage/Cost Spillovers

- **Coverage of workers and occupations is not universal.**

  - **Many coverage exclusions were never eliminated** (e.g., small employers, domestic workers, agricultural workers) (DOL, 2016, p. 9).
  - **Misclassifying workers as independent contractors** limits workers' access to workers' compensation and undermines incentives to provide a safe workplace (DOL, 2016, p. 20).
  - **The growth of alternative work arrangements** is also moving workers outside of covered employment, sometimes in high-risk jobs (Spieler, 2016, p. 100; Silverstein, 2010, p. 243).
  - **Uninsured employer funds have disappeared** in some states, leaving employees injured at uninsured employers without compensation if the employer has shut down or become insolvent (DOL, 2016, p. 19).

- **Underreporting of legitimate claims increases the burden of workplace injuries for employees**.

    - **Economically vulnerable workers often do not file claims following injury**. Employer pressure or retaliation, lack of legal knowledge, and a belief that the system is ineffective all discourage filing (Morantz, 2016, p. 46; DOL, 2016, p. 14).

- **Conditional on an injury occurring, employees have an incentive to report it as work-related, potentially leading to overreporting** (Lynch, 2016, p. 2).
- **The exclusion of specific injuries and diseases**, especially preexisting conditions and diseases of aging, increases system complexity and undermines coverage (DOL, 2016, p. 14). Examples include

    - MCC rules
    - apportionment to nonindustrial cause
    - restrictions on injury types
    - higher evidentiary standards
    - stricter time limits for filing claims, which particularly affect claims for cumulative trauma and occupational diseases.

- **Workers' compensation has never developed a satisfactory approach to determining permanent disability ratings** (DOL, 2016, pp. 15–16; Barth, 2010, p. 16).

    - **Impairment ratings** are not designed to capture disability and loss of productivity (Spieler, 2016, p. 80).
    - **American Medical Association guides** are not truly evidence-based and can reduce benefit adequacy (Swedlow, 2010, p. 206–207; Spieler, 2016, p. 43).
    - **Loss of fringe benefits and noneconomic losses can be significant** but are generally not compensated (Barth, 2010, p. 19).

- **Shifting cost burdens** to other social welfare programs, such as SSDI and Medicare, puts additional strain on those programs and reduces employer incentives to promote safety (DOL, 2016, p. 23; OSHA, 2015, p. 10; Morantz, 2016, p. 37).

Suggestions for Improvement

- Expand coverage to all workers, including volunteers and independent contractors (IAIABC, 2016b, p. 5).
- Reevaluate the definition of "employee" to include workers who have little control over the conditions in which they work (Spieler, 2016, p. 99).
- Simplify mechanisms for determining injury causation (IAIABC, 2016b, p, 5).
- Compensate injured workers for lost benefits (Barth, 2010, p. 19).

Internal Challenges

- **Stakeholders disagree about the goals and state of workers' compensation**. The willingness of large employers in Texas to accept tort liability in exchange for the opportunity to opt out of workers' compensation, for example, demonstrates the potential weakness of the grand bargain moving forward (Davoli, 2016, pp. 3–4).

- **State-level competition for business** has made cost control the primary goal for many legislative bodies when dealing with workers' compensation, resulting in a "race to the bottom" (Spieler, 2016, p. 92).

- **Legislative challenges in some states, including opt-out and coverage restrictions, threaten the viability of the system and adequacy of benefits** (IAIABC, 2016a, p. 2).

  - **There is the potential for dual denial** when workers with a noncompensable injury or illness are nonetheless unable to recover through the tort system (Spieler, 2016, pp. 40–41).

- **Second-injury funds have been eliminated in many states**, potentially making it risky for employers to hire disabled or older workers (Malooly, 2010, p. 54).

- There is a need for **sustained commitment to the residual marketplace**, as a poorly funded residual market can produce volatility in the voluntary market (Lipton and Ayres, 2010, p. 38).

- Political pressures on **monopolistic state insurers** can produce perverse incentives, leading to fraud or underpricing (Lynch, 2016, p. 3).

  - **The future of exclusive state funds depends on how rigorously they are managed**. If an exclusive state fund were to fail, it is extremely unlikely the political forces would be aligned to create a new one (Malooly, 2010, p. 53).

Suggestions for Improvement

- Consider federalization of system, which would create one set of rules for employers, carriers, attorneys, and workers; this change may result in less cost-shifting to other programs, such as SSDI, and eliminate the "race to the bottom" (IAIABC, 2016c, p. 5; Spieler, 2016, p. 99).

- Appoint a new national commission to study the workers' compensation system; reinstate federal tracking of changes in the workers' compensation system; establish standards that would trigger federal oversight if states fail to meet standards (DOL, 2016, p. 24).

- Develop an online dashboard allowing stakeholders to examine their program in terms of adequacy, equity, and efficiency; create a web-based clearinghouse to disseminate best practices (DOL, 2016, p. 25).

External Challenges

- **Changing labor relations and work arrangements are challenging system performance**, as workers' access to workers' compensation systems varies across classes of worker and nature of employment relationship.

  - **Temporary agency workers** often face confusion about coverage that may deter claiming (DOL, 2016, p. 20).
  - **Multiemployer worksites** (or **fissured workplaces**) may weaken prevention and rehabilitation functions of workers' compensation (OSHA, 2015, p. 8).

- **The decline in trade unions** weakens employee engagement with workers' compensation systems at the micro level and makes the systems more difficult to navigate for workers (Burton, 2016, p. 2).
- **The workers' compensation marketplace faces structural vulnerabilities**.
  - **The lingering effects of the financial crisis and increased labor force participation of older workers** puts more vulnerable workers into the risk pool (Lipton and Ayres, 2010, p. 38; Crum, 2010, p. 194).
  - **Concerns about lower investment yields** in the future may put upward pressure on premiums (Malooly, 2010, p. 49).

Suggestions for Improvement

- Continue to explore the use of portable benefits to expand coverage to temporary or multisite workers (Horejsh, 2017).

Promotion of Safety

- **Efforts to promote safety in the workplace through financial incentives also produce incentives to reduce legitimate claiming.**
  - **Behavior-based incentive programs** that reward workers for reporting no injuries ("injury-free periods") are commonplace and tend to suppress legitimate claims (Morantz, 2016, p. 39).
  - While **experience-rating is generally perceived to promote safety, international comparisons indicate this view is not universal**. Some stakeholders believe experience-rating may discourage legitimate claiming (OSHA, 2015, p. 9; Morantz, 2016, p. 23).
  - **Large deductible plans and self-insurance** incentivize employers to promote safety but also to encourage workers to not report legitimate claims (Spieler, 2016, p. 76).
- Despite general improvements in safety, **problems remain in safety promotion and oversight**. For example, American workers continue to be killed by hazards for which inexpensive protective measures have been available for years (Silverstein, 2010, p. 243).
  - Injury rates are not evenly distributed in the population. **Temporary, leased, or contingent workers face higher injury rates than their permanent counterparts** in the same industries (OSHA, 2015, p. 9).
- **Workers' compensation claims data have been shown to be a rich source of information to identify the causes of past injuries and develop ways to prevent future cases**. In addition to data analysis by the National Council on Compensation Insurance and the Workers Compensation Research Institute, private insurers, such as Liberty Mutual, and state agencies, such as Washington L&I, publish reports summarizing trends in costs, safety, and prevention. **Aggregating this information across insurers and states and using data to better understand injury causation have proven elusive**.

- The impact of **risk control systems on workplace safety** and health is not well understood (Wurzelbacher, 2017, p. 8).

Suggestions for Improvement

- Facilitate data sharing among state programs, insurance carriers, OSHA and state health and safety agencies, and state health departments to improve targeting of state and federal enforcement and loss control efforts of carriers (DOL, 2016, p. 25).
- Encourage insurers to promote employer adoption of comprehensive safety and health management programs (DOL, 2016, p. 25).
- Replace current "honor system" of workplace safety regulation with an accountability system, for example, requiring employers to implement a comprehensive health and safety program or obtain an annual certification of compliance with OSHA (Silverstein, 2010, p. 248).
- Consider expansion of tort remedies in situations where employers allow the persistence of known hazards (Spieler, 2016, p. 99).
- Expand antiretaliation protection for workers in all states, whether through amendments to federal law or state action (Spieler, 2016, p. 99).

Postinjury Outcomes

- **The system faces persistent challenges in facilitating return to work**. States vary widely in the use of active interventions to promote return to work. Consensus about best practices is elusive.

    - Stakeholders tend to **underinvest in workplace reintegration** because the costs of absence from work are distributed across many stakeholders (IAIABC Disability Management and Return to Work Committee, 2016, p. 37).
    - Physicians often **lack time and knowledge of workplace demands to make informed recommendations** about return to work. Programs such as COHE in Washington state are partially designed to improve provider knowledge of return-to-work requirements (Stapleton and Christian, 2016, p. 10).

- **Adequacy of TTD and, especially, PPD benefits have deteriorated in recent decades** due to cost-saving reforms, changes in disability rating, and other trends.

    - **Limits on TTD benefit duration** affect adequacy for the most severely disabled workers (DOL, 2016, pp. 9, 15).
    - **Waiting periods and delays in benefit payment can lead to hardship for workers without liquid wealth** (Spieler, 2016, p. 78).
    - **Adequacy for workers with multiple jobs** may vary widely by state, as some states count only the at-injury job when calculating the preinjury wage (Spieler, 2016, p. 78).
    - **Benefit caps and time limits** diminish adequacy in less visible ways (DOL, 2016, p. 22; IAIABC, 2016b, p. 3).
    - **Compensation for occupational diseases is often not adequate** (Spieler, 2016, p. 99).

Suggestions for Improvement

<u>Return to Work</u>

- Strengthen antidiscrimination legislation to enforce equal employment opportunities for people with disabilities. Penalties could be applied to employers who are unable to accommodate injured workers, or quotas could be used to promote retraining and reintegration (IAIABC Disability Management and Return to Work Committee, 2016, p. 37).
- Allow employers to deduct expenditures on workplace reintegration from taxes or workers' compensation payments (IAIABC Disability Management and Return to Work Committee, 2016, p. 38).
- Use matching funds to promote reintegration investments, or use wage subsidies to incentivize retention of injured workers (IAIABC Disability Management and Return to Work Committee, 2016, p. 38).
- Promote greater adoption of the International Classification of Functioning, Disability and Health (ICF) (IAIABC Disability Management and Return to Work Committee, 2016, p. 39).
- Introduce early reporting mechanisms so that patients receive rehabilitation services as soon as possible, and use flags early in the process to identify barriers to return to work. "Fit notes" from doctors may help communicate to return-to-work managers and employers what accommodations may be necessary to accommodate reintegration (IAIABC Disability Management and Return to Work Committee, 2016, pp. 39–40).
- Empower case managers with coordinating the medical and vocational rehabilitation process for the injured worker. Action plans and data dashboards for employers can improve efficacy (IAIABC Disability Management and Return to Work Committee, 2016, p. 41).
- Return-to-work efforts should follow the following guidelines: a holistic process, early intervention, individualized approaches, active participation of the injured worker, collaboration, use of qualified experts, and monitoring and evaluation (IAIABC Disability Management and Return to Work Committee, 2016, p. 89).
- Onsite health centers, including wellness, disease management, and stay-at-work (SAW) medical services, can successfully promote a culture of health and lower absence rates (North, 2010, p. 166).
- Advance research agenda on distribution of uncompensated wage losses: which workers are affected, systemic reasons for wage loss (versus randomness), and so forth (Hunt, 2010, p. 95).

<u>Benefit Adequacy</u>

- Revisit the national commission recommendations—new approaches to evidence-based research that can better predict earnings losses can assist in refining recommendations (Spieler, 2016, p. 98).
- Remove occupational diseases from grand bargain, and expose firms to tort liability in those cases (Spieler, 2016, p. 99).

Medical Management

- **Rising medical costs and poor integration with the medical system** strain resources and hurt outcomes.

    - **According to 2014 NASI estimates, medical benefits account for approximately half of workers' compensation (WC) costs nationally**. Despite medical cost increases, the workers' compensation system is too small to exert influence on the general medical system (McLaren and Baldwin, 2016, p. 5).
    - **Upward pressure on medical costs and related cost-control measures** threaten provider availability and incentives to provide quality care (Mueller and Harris, 2010, p. 149).
    - The system must address the challenge of **opioid use** (IAIABC, 2016c, p. 4).
    - **Technological trends, such as wearables, telemedicine, and genetics**, provide opportunities and challenges, notably privacy and integration with the administrative system (IAIABC, 2016c, p. 4).
    - **Uncertainty in the general health care system and efforts to implement universal health care** make the future role of workers' compensation unclear. (Steggert, 2010, pp. 75–76)

- **Medical cost-control efforts often use blunt tools** that are likely to impede access to needed care (Grabell and Berkes, 2015b; Spieler, 2016). These include

    - limits on office visits and benefit caps
    - time limits
    - fee schedules
    - limitations on physician choice.

- Efforts to implement **utilization review** have been hindered by **system complexity and regulatory scope issues** (IAIABC, 2016c, p. 4; Steggert, 2010, p. 63).

    - Efforts to make decisions based on **strict guidelines** have created a backlash among providers and workers (Mueller and Harris, 2010, p. 149).
    - Reviewers sometimes **lack all relevant information** related to a case, making adherence to guidelines difficult.

- Workers' compensation systems lack **demand-side controls on such costs as copayments, deductibles, and explicit enrollee contractual language** (Mueller and Harris, 2010, p. 137).

Suggestions for Improvement

- Push for universal health care, which would limit workers' compensation to indemnity payments only (IAIABC, 2016b, p. 5).
- Integrate workers' compensation health care payments with the general health care system (Spieler, 2016, p. 98).
- Implement utilization review with "teeth" (IAIABC, 2016b, p. 5).
- Expand the use of systematic reviews and meta-analyses to develop high-quality treatment guidelines (Mueller and Harris, 2010, p. 141).
- Promote the use and improvement of electronic medical records (Mueller and Harris, 2010, p. 150).

- Commit fully to the realization of outcomes-based care in the workers' compensation system (North, 2010, p. 175).

    - For employers, high-quality, efficient networks can reduce wasteful variations in practice standards and inefficiencies in the care delivery system.
    - For injured workers, evidence-based medical treatments provided by high-quality, efficient providers support their return to function.
    - For medical providers, pay-for-performance compensation with incentives will provide a clear value proposition that aligns quality standards with cost-saving activities.
    - For claims payors, care systems based on accurately measured outcomes are more inherently logical and easier to protect from manipulation than systems that are based primarily on processing benchmarks.
    - For all involved, focusing on improved medical outcomes aligns employers and claims payors with workers and providers in a shared goal that resonates with our society's sense of compassion and justice.

- Be more open to solutions outside the boundaries of the workers' compensation system (North, 2010, p. 176).

System Reputation/Outreach

- **Lack of trust in system threatens the long-term viability of the grand bargain** (DOL, 2016, p. 22).

    - There is a perception that employees have no **"skin in the game"** (IAIABC, 2016c, p. 4).
    - Stakeholders believe **more accountability is needed** across the board (North, 2010, p. 163).
    - **Participants, including injured workers, employers, insurers, and medical providers, need a better understanding of their roles and responsibilities** in the system (IAIABC, 2016a, p. 1).

- **The system has a bad reputation** and is seen as either harmful to workers or rife with fraud.

    - More and better **performance measurement** is needed (IAIABC, 2016a, p. 2).
    - More **transparency** is needed (IAIABC, 2016b, p. 3).
    - **A lack of communication with stakeholders and the public about the importance of an efficient workers' compensation system and the historical benefits of the grand bargain** exacerbates negative perspectives (IAIABC, 2016c, p. 2).

Suggestions for Improvement

- Introduce an ombudsman program for employers and employees to build trust among stakeholders (IAIABC, 2016b, p. 5).
- Raise awareness outside the industry of that workers' compensation has a role in economic growth and is not just another insurance product (IAIABC, 2016a, p. 1).
- Use technology to promote communication between parties (IAIABC, 2016b, p. 5).

Addendum: Supporting Quotations

Workers' Compensation Strengths

Workers' compensation has made a strong contribution to economic growth and has promoted workplace safety and stability.

> Workers' compensation was the first social insurance program adopted in the United States but today it is viewed mainly as an insurance product. The industry must raise awareness about the vital role workers' compensation plays in supporting economic growth. (IAIABC, 2016a, p. 1)

Workers' compensation systems are financially solvent now and into the future.

> Workers' compensation is financially secure, with funds to pay all claims. A majority of claims, 80–90%, are processed smoothly and result in minimal financial loss and quick return to work. (IAIABC, 2016a, p. 3)
>
> Frequency is continuing its downward trend.
>
> Indemnity costs are rising moderately.
>
> Accident year and calendar year combined ratios are favorable.
>
> Private carrier workers' compensation reserves are essentially adequate.
>
> Reforms in several states have been enacted. (Lipton and Ayres, 2010, p. 37)

Coverage is provided to most employees.

> With the exception of Texas, workers' compensation insurance coverage is mandatory for private-sector employers in all states, with limited exemptions for small employers and for workers in specific classifications, such as agricultural or domestic employees. (McLaren and Baldwin, 2016, p. 6)
>
> In 2014, workers' compensation covered an estimated 132.7 million U.S. workers, a 1.9 percent increase from the previous year. The number of workers covered increased steadily between 2010 and 2014, as the economy pulled out of the recession, such that 6.4 percent more workers were covered in 2014 than in 2010. Overall, workers' compensation coverage extended to an estimated 91 percent of the employed workforce and 97 percent of workers covered by unemployment insurance in 2014. (McLaren and Baldwin, 2016, p. 16)

Injury rates and average injury severity have declined over the last several decades.

> Over the past several decades, the U.S. has made great strides in reducing the incidence of workplace injuries, illnesses, and fatalities. (OSHA, 2015, p. 12)
>
> If one accepts the published data from OSHA, there has been a substantial decline in workplace injuries resulting in time lost from employment. Additionally, some jurisdictions have been reporting secular declines in compensable time loss cases. (Barth, 2010, p. 13)

<u>Culture of Safety</u>

We are also seeing the mix of claims change. Medical-only claims and serious long-term claims have declined but much less dramatically than the decline in less complex short-term claims . . . One often neglected trend that might account for a significant portion of this changing mix is the emergence of a new safety culture . . . We in the workers' compensation business tend to be too close to see the larger changes in society that can materially affect our business. (Malooly, 2010, p. 45)

While there were a number of influences contributing to the emergence of the safety culture, and experience rating of premium costs was clearly an important driver, the high costs in the 1980s and 1990s, driven in part by implementation of the recommendations of the National Commission, were clearly a contributor to the tremendous improvement in workplace safety. (Malooly, 2010, p. 48)

There has been a radical shift regarding expectations of safety at work . . . Today, workplace injuries are viewed as largely preventable by public health advocates, government regulators and many employers . . . This reconceptualization may have been partly responsible, in the 1980s and 1990s, for the legal struggle over the definition of intentional harm under the workers' compensation statutes. (Spieler, 2016, p. 61)

<u>Occupational Diseases</u>

Whatever shortcomings we find in the compensation of workers or survivors of those disabled or killed by occupational diseases, the state systems in general are more cognizant of such diseases and prepared to compensate for them. (Barth, 2010, p. 14)

Insurer-based prevention programs have demonstrated some success in reducing injuries.

According to a National Academy of Social Insurance (NASI) report, almost 76% of WC benefits in 2014 were paid by insurers rather than through self-insurance. Therefore, if a small employer receives safety and health information or services, in many cases it is through their WC insurer. WC insurer systems include underwriting, claims, and risk control departments that interact directly with a wide range of employers . . . Several insurers also offer programs to provide funds to insured employers to implement engineering controls and other prevention activities. (Wurzelbacher, 2017, p. 8)

Another distinguishing feature of European OSH regimes, as compared to that of the US, is their commonplace reliance on insurance-related incentives besides experience rating to promote OSH improvements. (Morantz, 2016, p. 43)

Unlike in the US, some of these schemes go beyond conventional experience rating and reward proactive, long-term strategies for accident and injury prevention. Many of these programs target a particular industry or small and medium-sized enterprises. (Morantz, 2016, p. 61)

Stakeholders have begun to take advantage of the rich data in the system, and claims administration has become more efficient over time.

Claims administration has become more efficient as automation has reduced paperwork. (IAIABC, 2016a, p. 1)

Recently the Ohio Bureau of Workers' Compensation collaborated with NIOSH-CWCS [Center for Workers' Compensation Studies] to produce [reports] to WA state. In a resulting study, this partnership demonstrated that a large state dataset of >1.2 million claims could be linked to external employment data to examine overall claims trends among state-insured private employers. (Wurzelbacher, 2017, p. 7)

Widespread commitment to the grand bargain is voiced by stakeholders within the system.

Much of the discussion was around the state-by-state nature of workers' compensation and how the grand bargain could be in tact [sic] in some states but not others. Generally, they felt the grand bargain had not been breached in most of the Central states but in some states it had . . . From a national level the system is not broken; however there was a general consensus that the grand bargain was under siege and that it was close to being breached in many states. It is a constant struggle to maintain balance between labor and management. (IAIABC, 2016d, p. 2)

Some state programs have demonstrated success in facilitating return to work.

Advances in medicine and understanding of return to work are helping improve outcomes for injured workers. More doctors and claim administrators are embracing the biopsychosocial model, understanding return to work and recovery is influenced by more than just a physical injury. Occupational health research informs safety practices, medical treatment, and return to work best practices which benefits everyone in the workforce. (IAIABC, 2016a, p. 3)

In its essence, COHE was designed to address the many behavioral bottlenecks that can stand in the way of achieving optimal medical recovery and return to work outcomes for WC claimants; the intent is to ensure maximally effective use of services and supports that were available in the absence of COHE, not to provide fundamentally new services and supports. Pilot testing that began in the early 2000s has demonstrated that COHE substantially reduces lost work time and long-term disability for WC claimants while more than paying for itself through lower WC expenditures. (Stapleton and Christian, 2016, p. 1)

[Marcos's activity coach] worked with him to make small strides each week in his activity level; walking to get the mail one day, then advancing to walking around the block a few days later. After five weeks in the program, he felt he was in control of his pain and his activity increased. He started cleaning the house and cooking meals. He even increased his physical therapy visits from one visit a week to three a week to help speed his recovery. He says the program gave him back his sanity and he has started his search for a new job. (IAIABC Disability Management and Return to Work Committee, 2016, p. 47)

Workers' Compensation Challenges

System Administration

The system is too complex, and variability in benefits, reporting requirements, forms, employee definitions, dispute processes, and other design features across jurisdictions creates confusion about what is compensable.

<u>Too Much Emphasis on Compliance, Not Outcomes</u>

> Most felt there were opportunities to promote uniformity across jurisdictions but felt it would be a challenging endeavor. Suggestions for places to begin were waiting periods, proof of coverage, benefit minimums and caps, notice posters, adoption of current CPT coding methodology and consistency in process for medical billing, adoption of formularies and treatment guidelines. (IAIABC, 2016b, p. 6)

> While many agreed shared agreement on the objectives would be desirable, there was more disagreement on the need for compliance or an enforcement mechanism. Many groups felt negatively about the need for compliance by an external body. (IAIABC, 2016b)

> A major unintended consequence of 25 years of changes in practice has been to make the workers' compensation system more difficult for all stakeholders to navigate. Employers, insurers and claims managers have all experienced increasing burdens of compliance. (North, 2010, p. 173)

> The workers' compensation system is too complex and the industry views some aspects (reporting, forms, etc.) as more focused on compliance with little or no benefit to employers and employees. (IAIABC, 2016a, p. 2)

> The state should ensure compliance by all parties; educate all parties; maintain equitable playing field for all. (IAIABC, 2016c, p. 3)

<u>Variation in Benefits</u>

> Levels of benefits for each category still differ considerably from one state to another. Temporary benefits, generally referred to as Temporary Total Disability (TTD) benefits and paid while the worker is healing and unable to work, are set at different levels in terms of weekly benefit levels and maximum duration of time to collect these benefits. (DOL, 2016, p. 9)

> This disparity grimly illustrates the geographic lottery that governs compensation for workplace injuries in America. Congress allows each state to determine its own benefits, with no federal minimums, so workers who live across state lines from each other can experience entirely different outcomes for identical injuries . . . Workers are awarded a portion of their wages up to the state maximum for the specified number of weeks assigned to each body part. But depending on those numbers, the final amounts can vary widely. (Grabell and Berkes, 2015a)

<u>Dispute Resolution</u>

We know the way that the systems are designed does not meet the needs of workers. For example, when an injured worker who is off work due to an injury or illness, and the workers' compensation claim is disputed, cash benefits and health care may be delayed until the dispute is resolved; leaving the injured worker with no income and putting tremendous pressure on them to settle claims for lesser amounts. A few states have come up with solutions for these kinds of problems . . . Maine has created mechanisms for payment of medical bills pending resolution of the workers' compensation claim . . . But even in these states, these solutions are the exception, not the rule. (DOL, 2016, pp. 21–22)

A company recently hired by the state auditor to review the system found that when disputes occur, WSI [North Dakota Workforce Safety & Insurance] relied entirely on out-of-state physicians mostly working for private companies that perform medical reviews for insurers. These doctors reversed the recommendations of workers' physicians 75 percent of the time, the September report by Sedgwick Claims Management Services found. (Grabell and Berkes, 2015b)

A third area where little or no progress has been made over the past 25 years, and indeed far longer, is the best way to minimize the time, costs, and uneven outcomes that arise in disputes over medical questions in dispute in compensation claims. I refer to a set of issues that include:

Establishing an impairment rating including assessing permanent total disability

Ability to return to work

Causation, particularly in occupational disease claims

Apportionment, including second injury fund liability

(Barth, 2010, p. 16)

90-percent agreement that system should reduce disputes and be less adversarial (IAIABC, 2016b, p. 1)

The state should ensure there is a balanced approach to resolving disputes. (IAIABC, 2016c, p. 3)

The state needs to provide a neutral forum for adjudication of disputes and enforce laws. (IAIABC, 2016d, p. 3)

System can be simplified with increased use of alternative employment dispute resolution and mediation. (IAIABC, 2016b, p. 5)

Do not make a rule/regulation about everything which will help eliminate disputes on how to interpret the rule/statute. (IAIABC, 2016b, p. 5)

The IAIABC is sponsoring a pilot project to develop a standardized workers' compensation dispute data model with the goal of measuring and comparing dispute drivers within the system. The pilot seeks to facilitate both intra- and inter-jurisdiction performance measures and inform leaders about dispute drivers and friction costs. (IAIABC, 2016a, p. 4)

Hand in hand with alternative dispute resolution is the ability to finally resolve and settle workers' compensation claims. A growing number of states have passed legislation that allows compromise and release of workers' compensation claims. The standards for approval, which vary from state to state, range from ensuring that the agreement is in the best interests of the injured worker to approving agreements presented without hearing. However, concerns remain that some compromise and release agreements will not be fair, even in cases where the injured worker is represented by counsel and purports to understand what he or she is doing. (Crum, 2010, p. 193)

Fee Restrictions for Attorneys

Changes in the processing and adjudication of claims have had enormous, though perhaps more hidden, impact on injured workers' access to benefits . . . Many of these legislative changes also lead to more complexity in proof requirements in claims, and therefore more complexity within the administrative process . . . Continuing growth in the complexity of litigation has contributed to delays, frustration and criticism of the systems . . . Lawyers on all sides are essential to help navigate the systems. But legislatures have enacted highly restrictive fee caps only for claimants' lawyers; there is not equivalent limitation on fees paid to lawyers who provide representation to insurance carriers and employers. (DOL, 2016, p. 17)

The crucial role of applicants' attorneys is illustrated by the effort to regulate applicants' attorneys' fees in the Florida workers' compensation program. The Florida workers' compensation statute was amended in 2003 to include an attorney's fee schedule that substantially reduced fees in many cases . . . The apparent reason for the Florida limitation on applicant attorneys' fees is the assumption that attorney involvement increases the amount of benefits paid to injured workers. But this assumption needs to be used with care. Casual inspection of workers' compensation data reveals that cash benefits tend to be higher in cases in which attorneys are involved, and there is a natural tendency to assume that attorneys are therefore responsible for the higher benefits. However, this assumption overlooks the likelihood that more serious injuries both result in higher benefits and attract lawyers, which means that the lawyers' involvement may not be a source of higher benefits. (Burton, 2016, p. 4)

Limited resources for system regulators prevent most states from playing an active role in helping workers navigate the system.

Another area consistently discussed was the lack of resources by state agencies to be effective. Without knowledgeable staff and appropriate resources (infrastructure, technology, etc.) administrative and regulatory progress is unlikely to be made. (IAIABC, 2016a, p. 4)

One theme echoed throughout the discussion was the need for funding and capable staff to administer regulatory agencies. Many agencies face staff turnover, recruitment, and retention challenges. It is hard to compete with the private industry with wages and benefits. Workers' compensation is a complex business and it requires a significant investment to train/educate new personnel. (IAIABC, 2016d, p. 4)

[Due to the economic downturn,] administrative agencies, insurers, and employers will be challenged to do more with less, at least in the first half of the next decade. This presents an opportunity to increase efficiencies and innovation in areas such as injury prevention, claims handling, disability management, and workforce development. (Crum, 2010, p. 194)

Coverage/Cost Spillovers

Coverage of workers and occupations is not universal.

> Employers are still not required to provide full coverage in many states to agricultural and domestic workers. (DOL, 2016, p. 9)

> Misclassification of workers as independent contractors is a growing phenomenon and results in their exclusion from much of the U.S. social safety net, including workers' compensation. Employers evade the payment of all payroll taxes as well as workers' compensation insurance premiums when they inappropriately classify their workers as non-employees, and the workers themselves are not covered when they are injured. (DOL, 2016, p. 20)

> It is true that most of our jobs are safer than they were 100 years ago. Despite this, the rhetorical and political parallels between 1900 and 2016 are troubling. Contingent attachment to the labor market is growing; proposals for elective workers' compensation laws are re-emerging; the reach of existing mandatory laws is being narrowed; the employment-at-will doctrine remains at the core of our employment law regime. (Spieler, 2016, p. 100)

> Many groups mentioned the need for a modernized and uniform definition of employee, especially in light of changing employment relationships. Each state defines employee differently, and often there are different definitions within a state for workers' compensation, unemployment, and taxation purposes. Some felt "employee" should be defined nationally but others believed it should stay a state-by-state issue. (IAIABC, 2016b, p. 1)

> Are volunteers covered? Are there employees who should be exempt? . . . What is "course of scope"? . . . What difference does it make about the location of where the accident occurred? (IAIABC, 2016b, p. 2)

Uninsured Employer Funds

> A second type of special fund is designed to cover injured workers whose employers fail to carry the requisite insurance . . . Without these funds, workers are left effectively without recourse. There are substantial penalties for employers who do not carry insurance, including elimination of immunity in tort, substantial fines and stop-work order. From the perspective of the injured worker, however, none of these penalties can substitute for a guarantee of no-fault wage replacement and medical care provided in a timely fashion. (DOL, 2016, p. 19)

Underreporting of legitimate claims increases the burden of workplace injuries for employees.

> US workers, employers, and physicians all have strong incentives to underreport workplace injuries. (Morantz, 2016, p. 46)

> Many workers who might be eligible for workers' compensation benefits never file claims . . . Explanations for this phenomenon vary. As discussed below, concerns about retaliation and stigmatization—enhanced by investigations regarding alleged fraud—undoubtedly discourage workers from filing claims. Undocumented or otherwise particularly vulnerable workers are particularly unlikely to file claims. Programs and policies of employers may themselves discourage reporting. (DOL, 2016, p. 14)

Since the early 1990s, workers' compensation claim frequency has shown a steady decline. This tracks a decline in injuries reported by the BLS. However, available evidence suggests that the number of reported workers' compensation claims greatly underestimates the actual number of workplace injuries eligible for benefits. (Boden and Spieler, 2010, p. 215)

Even among those who know of their right to receive benefits, some will fear that filing will trigger retaliation by employers, who may lay them off, place them in undesirable jobs or shifts, eliminate pay raises, and so on. (Boden and Spieler, 2010, p. 218)

There is a tendency to oversimplify the process of claims filing by dividing claims into two clearly defined groups, eligible (or worthy) claims and ineligible claims . . . [I]n this view, systems must be designed to exclude "ineligible" claims . . . The issues may be considerably more complex than this view would suggest. Barriers may discourage or exclude both clearly work-related injuries and injuries that fall in a gray area of potential claims. (Boden and Spieler, 2010, pp. 218–219)

Conditional on an injury occurring, employees have an incentive to report it as work related, potentially leading to overreporting.

Given an injury, the injured or ill person has an incentive to claim the malady is work-related. A work injury requires no out-of-pocket expenses, and the injured person will receive compensation while they recover. Both confer economic advantages not available in health insurance. (Lynch, 2016, 2)

There are also incentives for workers and/or medical providers to over-report injuries or illnesses as work-related. The 100 percent coverage of medical costs under workers' compensation creates incentives for both groups to identify a work-related cause when the etiology of an injury or illness is uncertain. Workers also have incentives to report injuries as work related if they can receive higher disability benefits from workers' compensation than from a private disability plan or state unemployment insurance. (McLaren and Baldwin, 2016, pp. 47–48)

The exclusion of specific injuries and diseases, especially preexisting conditions and diseases of aging, increases system complexity and undermines coverage.

In the historic view of workers' compensation, workers were to be compensated if the workplace event aggravated a preexisting condition. Many states have now enacted higher standards for causation, requiring that the work be the "major contributory cause" of the workers' disability. As a result, workers who enter a workplace with preexisting disabilities—whether caused by work or not—may be denied compensation, despite the fact that they were able to perform their jobs before they were injured. (DOL, 2016, p. 14)

Some states, like California, that have not adopted the major contributing cause standard discussed above instead require physicians to "apportion" the amount of impairment between work and non-work causes . . . Pre-existing impairments are thus excluded from the rating for compensation purposes. This process sets the amount of compensation at a level below the level of actual impairment—and it leads inevitably to increases in the complexity of evaluation and the potential for more litigation. (DOL, 2016, p. 15)

Another group agreed it was not enough to have a standard definition of employee, there is a need for consistency in what conditions are covered under workers' compensation (i.e. mental, physical). (IAIABC, 2016b, p. 2)

Workers' compensation has never developed a satisfactory approach to determining permanent disability ratings.

In the last two decades, the requirements to qualify for [PPD benefits] have become more stringent and the length of time the benefits are provided has shrunk. Some states have cut off these benefits at retirement age. Some jurisdictions have set a maximum duration amount for these benefits, despite the permanency of disability. It is these workers—who are hurt the worst or who are most disabled as a result of occupationally-caused injuries or illnesses—who are most likely to turn to other social benefit programs, particularly SSDI. (DOL, 2016, pp. 15–16)

Most persons familiar with workers' compensation recognize the difficulties associated with permanent partial disability compensation. Around the world, systems struggle to find an approach that is fair to injured workers and provides incentives for them to be reintegrated into the labor force. Moreover, achieving cost-efficient outcomes and both horizontal and vertical equity (equal treatment of equals and unequal treatment of those with varying levels of disability) remains elusive . . . What is needed is research that can demonstrate which methods of compensation can come closest to meeting some of these criteria. (Barth, 2010, p. 16)

It is possible that creating a stable and precise disability evaluation and payment model is an unrealistic goal for any jurisdiction over the long term. Estimating future earning power depends on shifting proportions of information about the known (average wages of similar workers, industry and demographics information) and unknown (domestic and global workforce changes, productivity, innovation, etc.). The best-case scenario may lie within the very process that has been in play for the last 100 years—an iterative cycle of social policy decision making, experimentation, assessment, and course correction. (Swedlow, 2010, pp. 210–211)

In addition, the problem of assessing permanent disability has plagued the workers' compensation program since its inception. The current state programs are not designed to fully replace earnings lost as the result of an injury. Permanent total disability benefits are rarely awarded and are capped in various ways; these cases are also often classified as partial disability cases and settled without any real review of the long-term employment possibilities for the injured worker. Partial benefits are calculated in a range of ways, none of which are designed to replace lifetime earnings losses for injured workers. (Spieler, 2017, p. 80)

Shifting cost burdens to other social welfare programs, such as SSDI and Medicare, puts additional strain on those programs and reduces employer incentives to promote safety.

As permanent disability benefits are eroded, workers with significant permanent disabilities that make it difficult for them to function in the labor market turn to SSDI. (DOL, 2016, p. 23)

The number of Social Security Disability Insurance (SSDI) beneficiaries and the amount of benefits paid by that program has also grown dramatically in recent years. An accumulating body of evidence shows that at least part of the growth in SSDI benefit payments is attributable to the program's subsidy for work injuries and illnesses. (OSHA, 2015, p. 10)

If a US worker does file a claim, a great deal may hinge on whether her employer deems the claim to be compensable . . . If the employee's claim is denied . . . her economic situation is likely to deteriorate far more rapidly than would that of a similarly-situated worker in a comparator country [Canada, Australasia, Europe], who can rely on publicly-provided health insurance and more robust forms of government-provided income support . . . Unless the employee is insured by a private long-term disability plan or can draw on family support, she may have few alternatives but to apply to SSDI. (Morantz, 2016, p. 37)

Variation in the programmatic dimensions of workers' compensation systems across US states is dwarfed by the disparity between the insurance available to federal employees and to those available to the other 98% of US workers. The Federal Employees' Compensation Act (FECA) program provides federal employees with full salary (with no waiting period) for the first 45 days after injury. (Morantz, 2016, pp. 21–22)

Internal Challenges

Stakeholders disagree about the goals and state of workers' compensation.

There is disagreement about the current state of workers' compensation in the United States. Some believe the grand bargain is fraying, with competition across states focused on cost at the expense of injured workers. Others argue the grand bargain continues to evolve and the system is working relatively well as it is fully funded, stable in many states and that the vast majority of claims are settled without hearing processes. (IAIABC, 2016a, p. 2)

Workers' advocates view workers' compensation as a critically necessary social benefit program . . . The view is that the current system is woefully inadequate, both procedurally and substantively, and it is growing worse as states race to the bottom and the increasingly fissured workplace creates more work without any employment protections. (Spieler, 2017, p. 92)

Contrary to Emily Spieler's admonition "As long as tort immunity is strong, the Grand Bargain is alive and well", Texas employers have not been restrained by risk of injured employee liability by embracing a fault-based system; especially larger employers, like Wal-Mart, who apparently have assessed the financial risks of tort liability against the costs of a workers' compensation benefit system, regardless of the impact those work injuries may have on their employees or the cost-shift to Texas taxpayers. (Davoli, 2016, pp. 3–4)

Notwithstanding rhetoric often espoused that the principle mission of the "industry" is the welfare and best interests of the injured worker, reality experienced from battles in the trenches over ever-eroding benefits amidst ever-increasing and more onerous administrative and dispute resolution proceedings, when coupled with increasing medical and employer costs in many states, makes a more compelling argument supporting a higher priority for survival and profitability in the "industry" rather than the welfare of injured workers and their families. (Davoli, 2016, p. 2)

Legislative challenges in some states, including opt-out and coverage restrictions, threaten the viability of the system and adequacy of benefits.

Opting out of workers' compensation is not entirely new. Starting in the 1990s, 12 states developed "carve out" options under which employers and unions are authorized to negotiate an alternative workers' compensation system, arguably to speed up claims administration and dispute resolution. These options were primarily supported and utilized by the construction industry, where injuries are frequent and workers' compensation costs are generally high, and were subject to negotiation with the trade unions. (DOL, 2016, p. 19)

The plans in both Texas and Oklahoma give employers almost complete control over the medical and legal process after workers get injured. Employers pick the doctors and can have workers examined—and reexamined—as often as they want. And they can settle claims at any time. Workers must accept whatever is offered or lose all benefits. If they wish to appeal, they can—to a committee set up by their employers. (Grabell and Berkes, 2015c)

There was concern about "opt-out" and alternatives to workers' compensation, believing it did not equally serve the interests of employers and employees. Participants were critical of recent reports and news stories about the state of workers' compensation systems, noting inaccuracies and misinterpretation. (IAIABC, 2016a, p. 3)

Opt-out may be moving away from the grand bargain. (IAIABC, 2016d, p. 2)

Where important changes are made in state programs, some may label them as "reforms"; they are likely to be the result of employer and/or insurer pressures to assist them. (Barth, 2010, p. 17)

Dual Denial

States have abandoned the long accepted rule regarding aggravation of pre-existing injuries. In the past, employers "took workers as they found them." This rule is being supplanted in one state after another with rules that require a worker to demonstrate that the workplace event was the "major contributing cause"—or equivalent language—to the disability. Workers who cannot meet this standard are excluded from obtaining benefits—despite the fact that it was the workplace injury that precipitated the inability to continue to work. These workers are sometimes also dually excluded: unable to obtain compensation, but also barred from bringing negligence actions. (Spieler, 2017, pp. 40–41)

Second-injury funds have been eliminated in many states, potentially making it risky for employers to hire disabled or older workers.

Initially created in order to promote the employment of people with disabilities after World War II, many states eliminated [special injury funds] in the more recent period, arguing they were no longer necessary with the development of laws prohibiting discrimination against people with disabilities. In several states, these funds were closed out except for injuries or claims prior to a specified date . . . The combination of elimination of these funds and the exclusion of conditions with multiple causes means that an increasing number of workers with conditions that are related to—though perhaps not wholly or principally caused by—their current work cannot obtain benefits. (DOL, 2016, pp. 18–19)

As more workers remain in the workforce longer, more workers will come to the job with preexisting conditions that might discourage employers from hiring them. As the economy recovers, the underlying worker shortage will again become apparent. Older workers will both need to work and want to continue to be productively employed. A rethinking of the role of second injury funds may result. (Malooly, 2010, p. 54)

There is a need for sustained commitment to the residual marketplace, as a poorly funded residual market can produce volatility in the voluntary market.

The environment needs to foster the effective functioning of a residual market mechanism. Not only is rate adequacy important in the voluntary market, but history has shown that an inadequately funded residual market can have a wide-reaching effect on the workers' compensation system. (Lipton and Ayres, 2010, p. 38)

A second type of special fund is designed to cover injured workers whose employers fail to carry the requisite insurance . . . Without these funds, workers are left effectively without recourse . . . But in almost half of the states, there is no fund to provide this cushion for workers—and when employers have shut down or become insolvent, it is the injured worker who may be left out in the cold (DOL, 2016, pp. 18–19)

Political pressures on monopolistic state insurers can produce perverse incentives, leading to fraud or underpricing.

If managers of a state fund succumb to political pressure and consistently underprice the insurance even by a small amount, immense unfunded obligations can be incurred. Sooner or later, this economic reality must be addressed. (Malooly, 2010, p. 53)

It is often difficult to divine [the incentives of monopolistic workers' compensation insurers], because monopolistic carriers are quasi-governmental in nature. They aren't driven to maximize profits . . . That does not mean such carriers automatically operate altruistically. They are vulnerable to political pressures, and those pressures can take interesting forms. The near monopoly that is the Ohio Bureau of Workers' Compensation (insuring approximately two-thirds of all employees in the state), for example, in 2005 invested $50 million of its surplus in gold coins sold by a politically connected coin dealer. (Lynch, 2016, p. 3)

External Challenges

Changing labor relations and work arrangements are challenging system performance.

Workers who are hired by staffing or temporary work agencies often are unsure about their rights—to the point that new "right to know" laws for temporary workers have been enacted, and specifically require that a worker be told who the workers' compensation carrier is, in case they are injured. (DOL, 2016, p. 20)

If several firms employ workers at the same site, and employers do not actively collaborate to ensure safe workplaces, all workers at the site may be at a higher risk of injury . . . Misclassifying workers increases the likelihood of work injuries through two mechanisms. First, by misclassifying wage employees as independent contractors, employers do not have to worry about the OSHA requirement to provide a safe workplace, since OSHA law does not cover the self-employed. Second, these employers avoid paying workers' compensation insurance premiums (as well as unemployment insurance and other benefits and taxes). (OSHA, 2015, p. 8)

<u>Decline in Union Representation</u>

From the standpoint of workers, the deleterious developments in the workers' compensation program in recent decades has in part been due to the decline in the union movement. (Burton, 2016, p. 2)

Workers are more vulnerable to retaliation without unions—and few workers in the private sector are now unionized. (DOL, 2016, p. 14)

The workers' compensation marketplace faces structural vulnerabilities.

Contraction of the U.S. economy will lead to a decline in net written premium for the industry . . . While we expect frequency to continue to decrease as it has in prior recessions, the depth of this recession could take us into uncharted waters. (Lipton and Ayres, 2010, p. 38)

The largest segment of our population—the baby boomers—will represent the largest segment of our workforce. The aging workforce, baby boomers, and older workers who are retiring from the workforce much later, present challenges in terms of susceptibility to injury, lengthier recovery times from injury, and barriers to return to work. (Crum, 2010, p. 194)

The future for investment returns is much more uncertain than it had been in the recent past. This will have significant effects on the price of workers' compensation insurance, at least in the near future. (Malooly, 2010, p. 49)

Promotion of Safety

Efforts to promote safety in the workplace through financial incentives also produce incentives to reduce legitimate claiming.

In theory, the worker's incentives at the first moment (before hire) are straightforward: she has strong incentives to acquire information about job hazards and to take this information into account when bargaining over wages. In practice, however, the employee's consideration of OSH-related hazards ex ante will likely depend on the success of regulators and unions in raising awareness of OSH issues. (Morantz, 2016, p. 9)

<u>Behavior-Based Incentive Programs</u>

Recent trends suggest that US firms are responding strongly to [incentives to reduce premiums]. For example, "behavior-based" incentive programs that reward workers for reporting no injuries or that penalize workers who do report them are commonplace in the US. Although they are typically justified as a means to reduce risk-bearing moral hazard, these programs have been repeatedly criticized by OSHA—although not, to date, categorically banned—on the grounds that "an incentive program that focuses on injury and illness numbers often has the effect of discouraging workers from reporting an injury or illness." Deterring workers from reporting injuries in the first place is perhaps the least costly way of reducing workers' compensation costs. (Morantz, 2016, p. 39)

Experience-Rating

While lacking a financial incentive to train temporary employees, employers do have a financial incentive to contract out their most dangerous jobs. For many employers, the state's workers' compensation premiums are experience-rated, meaning that, in general, employers with fewer claims pay lower premiums. In theory, this experience rating provides some financial incentive for employers to invest in safety to prevent injuries and lower insurance premiums. By assigning workers employed by a staffing agency to the most dangerous tasks, host employers may hope to avoid higher premiums. (OSHA, 2015, p. 9)

There is considerable international dissensus regarding the costs and benefits of experience rating. While proponents tout the efficiency-enhancing properties of experience rating, which in theory induces firms to internalize the costs of occupational hazards, skeptics have expressed the concern that experience rating incentivizes companies to underreport injuries and that the most common forms (which rely on lagged data) do not reward firms quickly enough for innovative prevention measures. The fact that a number of comparator countries do not experience rate demonstrates that the critical perspective holds sway in some industrialized nations. (Morantz, 2016, p. 23)

Large Deductible Plans and Self-Insurance

Benefits are financed through various insurance mechanisms. In all but four states, employers purchase coverage from private insurance carriers or self-insure after providing some evidence of financial capacity. Increasingly, employers purchase plans with large deductibles, so that initial claims' costs are paid directly by the employer. These employers, as well as self-insured employers, generally engage third party administrators to manage claims. Self-insurance creates larger incentives for employers to manage the costs of claims and to assist workers in returning to work—but it increases incentives to discourage the filing of claims in the first place. (Spieler, 2017, p. 76)

Despite general improvements in safety, problems remain in safety promotion and oversight.

American workers continue to be killed by hazards for which inexpensive protective measures have been available and well recognized for hundreds, and in some cases thousands, of years. For example, every week one or more workers are killed in trench cave-ins despite the fact that nearly 2,500 years ago Herodotus described how the Phoenician army protected its soldiers by simple sloping trenches used in the Persian Wars. (Silverstein, 2010, p. 243)

While we can improve OSHA compliance by taking advantage of the existing authority inherent in the act and fine tuning it, its objectives would be best met by a more substantial redesign, replacing the honor system with a system requiring that employers implement comprehensive health and safety programs and receive annual certification and compliance. (Silverstein, 2010, p. 235)

<u>Temporary, Leased, or Contingent Workers</u>

The increased employment of temporary workers also increases the risk of work injuries. Temporary workers, often employed through staffing agencies, are generally at the worksite for shorter time periods. Researchers in the state of Washington found temporary workers in the construction and manufacturing sectors had twice the rate of injuries of workers in standard employment relationships . . . New workers often lack adequate safety training and are likely to be unfamiliar with the specific hazards at their new workplace. As a result, new workers are several times more likely to be injured in the first months on the job than workers employed for longer periods. Consistent with these findings, OSHA has investigated numerous incidents in recent months in which temporary workers were killed on their first days on the job. (OSHA, 2015, p. 9)

Aggregating claims information across insurers and states and using data to better understand injury causation and prevention have proven elusive.

<u>Risk Control Systems</u>

WC insurers offer onsite prevention services and programs for insured employer risk control. Collected employer data may include information on types of hazards present in the workplace, safety-health programs and controls in place, and return-to-work programs to reduce injury-illness severity. Despite the potential use of non-claims WC data in guiding prevention efforts, no known studies have systematically reviewed the types of employer risk control reports that WC insurers collect nor examined data quality and comparability of reports across carriers. (Wurzelbacher, 2017, p. 8)

Postinjury Outcomes

The system faces persistent challenges in facilitating return to work.

Across all states, we found that workers who had a second absence were much more likely to indicate that they had returned to work too soon after their injuries—66 percent of workers across the 15 study states who had a second absence responded that they returned to work too soon, compared with 35 percent of those who did not have a second absence. (Savych and Thumula, 2017, p. 28)

In particular, the percent of prime-age men who report that they are ill or disabled has grown from less than two percent in the late 1960s to about three percent in 1983 and to nearly five percent by 2003. Is it possible that workers' compensation cases are indicating the same phenomenon? If injured workers are more likely to decide that they do not want to return to work, we should not label that as the fault of the workers' compensation system. (Hunt, 2010, p. 94)

Workers' compensation systems have better performance if injured workers achieve more complete physical recovery from their injuries. System features and the delivery of medical care can interact with physical recovery to influence workers' ability to return to work. (Belton, 2010, p. 111)

[Workers' compensation settlements] not only may substantially discount the long-term effects of workplace injury, they also include provisions that terminate medical care and often bar the injured worker from seeking to return to work with the pre-injury employer. (DOL, 2016, p. 18)

Effective return to function is a societal obligation that must be embraced by employers, regulators, injured workers, co-workers, carriers, caregivers, and vendors; all the parties that play active roles in an injured person's life are responsible for helping them return to a productive, contributory role in society. (IAIABC Disability Management and Return to Work Committee, 2016, p. 9)

Workers are sometimes perceived as malingering, not interested in returning to work or function, or even seeking fraudulent opportunities. The reality is that workers often return to function, and work, before the insurance carrier is even aware of the injury . . . Unions are often seen as defending a worker's entitlement to compensation and resisting early return to work at the expense of the worker's functional recovery. These perceptions cause employers, insurance companies, and co-workers to question the legitimacy of the impairment and absence from work . . . Employers are sometimes seen as uncaring, only being interested in reducing their insurance costs. Many employers carry the belief that they are not prepared to take a worker back to work until they are 100% recovered from their injury and are financially able to do so . . . Caregivers can be perceived as unwilling participants in a return to work program . . . Insurance companies are perceived as interested in profitability at the expense of the well-being of the injured person. (IAIABC Disability Management and Return to Work Committee, 2016, p. 11)

Employers sometimes mistakenly believe they should wait for a full release to work from the worker's medical provider or that they should not contact the worker while he or she is in treatment due to health care privacy concerns . . . these views damage the employer's credibility with the worker. (IAIABC Disability Management and Return to Work Committee, 2016, p. 16)

Trust in the workplace is one of the most important predictors of return to work. (IAIABC Disability Management and Return to Work Committee, 2016, pp. 17–18)

Some insurers may see a conflict in return to work and claim settlement as the prevention of future claim exposures is considered to financially beneficial. However, if the insurer can return an injured worker back to a greater level of function or earnings via modified duty than he or she would have otherwise experienced, the injured worker's impairment is lessened and earning capacity increased. (IAIABC Disability Management and Return to Work Committee, 2016, p. 28)

Alleviating Provider Constraints

The COHEs also conduct activities that are not specific to individual claims, but are designed to improve workforce retention practices by all stakeholders in the community. Most notably, COHEs help to develop and pilot emerging best practices and provide technical assistance to help providers implement them. Three current examples are:

Training physical and occupational therapists in use of the Progressive Goal Attainment Program (PGAP), an activity coaching/motivational intervention;

Develop and use of the Functional Recovery Questionnaire (FRQ) and Interventions (FRI), a six-question screening tool to identify workers at high risk for long-term disability, with a follow-up protocol initiated by HSCs [health service coordinators] to develop and execute an intervention plan that includes components such as PGAP, advisor referral, and functional recovery interventions; and

Three pilot projects concerning four new best practices for workers requiring surgery. (Stapleton and Christian, 2016, p. 10)

The adequacy of TTD and, especially, PPD benefits have deteriorated in recent decades.

For workers whose claims are accepted or approved, the amount of benefits they receive has been limited through various legislative changes. The National Commission's benchmark for wage replacement adequacy (two-thirds of lost earnings, at least up to a maximum of the state average weekly wage) . . . has never been met. (DOL, 2016, p. 15)

The general consensus was adequacy of indemnity benefits was as close to pre-injury wages as possible and allow a person to remain in the same socio-economic class. Another group said adequate indemnity benefits should be more than just survival; they should be adequate to maintain a similar lifestyle and replace it as close to possible future earning losses as well as include the loss of pension, 401k and other benefits contributions. The system needs to redefine "covered wages" to calculate for [sic] these benefits. (IAIABC, 2016b, p. 3)

How can the savings due to the efficiency of future win-win systems be returned to injured workers in the form of benefit adequacy without unbalancing the system and reverting to attorney-driven litigation for dollars? (Steggert, 2010, p. 75)

Any jurisdiction's ability to deliver benefits depends on the choice of disability rating system as well as the method of implementation and administration—all of which flow from underlying social policy decisions on adequacy, equity, and efficiency. (Swedlow, 2010, p. 200)

Waiting Periods and Liquidity Constraints

The problems with the adequacy of cash benefits begin as soon as workers are off work because of an injury. For those workers who only receive temporary benefits for a short time, the waiting period required to trigger wage replacement benefits means that they are left without income for a portion of their absence; the benefits for the initial days is only restored if their absence exceeds a specified period. . . . What this means for individual workers and their families is that, in many situations, they cannot meet household expenses even if they qualify for benefits. (Spieler, 2017, p. 78)

Multiple Job Holding

For those workers who work several jobs—arguably a growing phenomenon—the lost earnings from other jobs may not be covered by the temporary benefits . . . Again, this varies by state. (Spieler, 2017, p. 78)

<u>Benefit Caps and Time Limits</u>

The combination of unfiled legitimate claims, benefit caps, barriers to accessing medical care, and potentially inadequate settlements of permanent disability claims together mean that the direct costs of worker morbidity and death are transferred away from the employers, decreasing any direct economic incentive to invest in safety. (DOL, 2016, p. 22)

Many people agreed that maximum benefit caps were not equitable. Some commented it was also not equitable to have different classes of workers (i.e. Full-time vs. Part-time workers) or those with employment contracts would receive different kinds of benefits. In addition, time limits restrictions on certain kinds of indemnity benefits (i.e., TTD) were not equitable. (IAIABC, 2016b, p. 3)

Arbitrary limits on the number of weeks that temporary total disability benefits are available in a claim . . . have been instituted or shortened; This provision was successfully challenged when the Florida Supreme Court recently held a 104 week limit on these benefits to be unconstitutional under the Florida state constitution. Employers in some states are apparently forbidden to provide longer benefits, under threat of audit or fine, even if they are willing. (DOL, 2016, p. 15)

Many of these changes are insidious—they occur without being obvious to observers because they do not involve bright line changes such as a reduction in the weekly benefit rate paid to an injured worker. (Spieler, 2017, p. 39)

<u>Occupational Diseases</u>

The failure of workers' compensation to compensate most victims of occupational diseases also needs to be addressed. If workers' compensation systems are not able to compensate occupational diseases that develop over time, then these diseases should be removed from the "bargain" and employers should, when appropriate, be liable in tort. (Spieler, 2017, p. 99)

Medical Management

Rising medical costs and poor integration with the medical system strain resources and hurt outcomes.

Medical management and integration with the general health care system is a challenge. Workers' compensation makes up just over 1% of the overall health care spend in the United States which leaves it with little leverage to influence medical practices on a large scale. (IAIABC, 2016a, p. 4)

One broad lesson for policymakers derived from WCRI's [Workers Compensation Research Institute's] worker outcomes studies is that access or satisfaction problems are not fixed by paying more for medical care. (Belton, 2010, p. 107)

The efficacy of workers' compensation medical care in some systems appears to be significantly worse than that in general health. (Mueller and Harris, 2010, p. 136)

In WC there are a large number of minor claims, which may continue to be managed adequately using a version of the current episodic model. These are frequently medical-only claims or claims with short periods of temporary disability. However, the major cost drivers in the system are now claims with prolonged care and disability. While a few of these claims are due to catastrophic injuries, most are related to some type of chronic pain and repeated but often ineffective treatment. (Mueller and Harris, 2010, p. 139)

Progress in the management of occupational medical care has been largely driven by the implementation of techniques first developed in the non-occupational health care arena . . . We must continue to borrow unashamedly from the entire health care and health insurance community in our efforts to improve medical management. For example, over the past few years, non-occupational group health plans have implemented initiatives to improve the quality and efficiency of care through incentive programs, called "Pay for Performance." (North, 2010, pp. 175–186)

Whereas prescription drug costs have historically been minimal in the context of overall workers' compensation expenses, current costs are approaching 20 percent of total medical costs. (Steggert, 2010, p. 64)

Lack of incentives for medical providers to focus on treatments that offer best outcomes. (IAIABC, 2016c, p. 4)

Will future workers' compensation systems be threatened and/or become extinct if and when universal health coverage comes to America? Will labor and management be aligned over whether workers' compensation systems should or should not be integrated into universal health care? How will workers' compensation systems deal with indemnity benefit delivery and be win-win while minimizing litigation if and when health care becomes "free choice" in the universal health care era? (Steggert, 2010, p. 76)

Comment that an all payer health care system would change workers' comp into an indemnity program only . . . needs to be consideration of the consequences of delinking medical benefits and indemnity. (IAIABC, 2016b, p. 2)

Medical cost-control efforts often use blunt tools that are likely to impede access to needed care.

Fee Schedules

Other states, like Illinois and Delaware, have enacted more subtle changes, such as placing strict caps on payments to doctors and hospitals through medical fee schedules. The measures help control costs, but, critics say, they also cause some doctors to stop taking workers' comp patients. (Grabell and Berkes, 2015b)

Discussion groups were asked to discuss if "flexible and adaptable" were at odds with "stable and predictable"—which is often the desire of many within the industry. Opinions varied greatly in answering this question, with some regulators believing stable and predictable was more desirable . . . Another comment was that stable does not mean static (example of TX fee schedule = stable but not static). (IAIABC, 2016b, p. 2)

About 80 percent of the jurisdictions with workers' compensation fee schedules (36 of 44) based their maximum reimbursement rates on relative value units . . . The administration of the usual, customary, and reasonable charges as a basis for reimbursement rates requires substantial resources on the part of the state agencies, both for development of a sufficient and accurate database of charges or fees in the local communities and for timely updates to the database to capture changes in the prevailing charges or reimbursements and in the utilization of new procedures. (Fomenko and Liu, 2016, p. 18)

<u>Physician Choice</u>

For example, previous WCRI research on the impact of provider choice in four states indicates that the workers' ability to choose their primary provider or to select a new provider resulted in higher overall satisfaction with medical care compared to when the employer chose the provider. (Belton, 2010, p. 105)

Increasing medical costs have also led to a wide range of statutory changes and health care management interventions intended to slow these rising costs . . . For example, the right of worker-patients to choose their treating physician has been significantly restricted: in at least thirteen states the employer chooses the physician, at least initially. In some of these states, no provision is made for workers to switch to physicians of their own choice without approval from the employer or insurer. Not surprisingly, workers and their advocates view some of these restrictions with hostility. (Spieler, 2017, p. 72)

Efforts to implement utilization review (UR) have been hindered by system complexity and regulatory scope issues.

Utilization review is too cumbersome. (IAIABC, 2016c, p. 4)

Without being critical given the well-intentioned proliferation of UR programs, the effectiveness of some state programs has been undermined by a combination of complex design and/or regulatory scope issues. Additionally, some payors' have, in my opinion, missed the boat by making "black-and-white" UR decisions based on strict adherence to guidelines. Such inappropriate decision making has created a backlash among providers. (Steggert, 2010, p. 63)

Systems that have not met their full potential, despite legislative intent, tend to have 1) ineffective UR review protocols or structures and/or 2) no effective enforcement or adjudicatory mechanism. (Steggert, 2010, p. 64)

Medical cost control measures such as utilization review, medical fee schedules, and managed-care organizations were all thought to be methods which would stabilize medical costs. The actual evidence is mixed. (Mueller and Harris, 2010, p. 136)

Guidelines specifically aimed at the workers' compensation population and used for utilization review and case management do appear to be effective in various areas. Evidence-based utilization review was mandated in California in 2003 . . . A recent analysis of medical care utilization demonstrated a 68.6 percent decline in claims with chiropractic care with a 90 percent drop in chiropractic claims over the 24 visit cap from 2002 to 2006. (Mueller and Harris, 2010, pp. 146–147)

Utilization review is often viewed by providers as time consuming and punitive, and as often practiced is not the most satisfactory or successful manner of controlling costs. If providers adhere to an evidence-based medical home model, payors should automatically pay for most care; only care outside of guideline recommendations would require review. (Mueller and Harris, 2010, p. 152)

Workers' compensation systems lack demand-side controls on such costs as copayments, deductibles, and explicit enrollee contractual language.

Workers' compensation systems also lack demand-side controls such as co-payments, deductibles, and explicit enrollee contractual language common to group health and federal program plans. In addition, many workers' compensation jurisdictions lack impartial, physician-based dispute resolution systems and rely upon adversarial processes made up of appeals board judges and "dueling docs." (Mueller and Harris, 2010, p. 137)

System Reputation/Outreach

Lack of trust in system threatens the long-term viability of the grand bargain.

Low benefits and transfers of costs adversely affect the social and psychological environment for working people who already face many challenges in the current economy. Distrust—on all sides, in individual claims, with regard to systemic issues and the political process—characterizes almost every state program and undoubtedly contributed to workers' decisions not to file claims and to employers' decisions to fight claims. (DOL, 2016, p. 22)

Employers are responsible for tending the contract and should make sure the system adapts to the changing workplace, workforce, and kind of work. Employers need to make sure their workplaces are safe and have a responsibility to report injuries . . . Employees need to know what their benefits [sic] under workers' compensation. They have a duty to be safe and report unsafe practices at work. (IAIABC, 2016c, p. 3)

Those who participate in the system (i.e. [injured workers]) have no "skin in the game" (i.e. there is no incentive for them to comply with medical treatment or get back to work). (IAIABC, 2016c, p. 4)

On another front, the suspicion—and too often the reality—of fraud continues to compromise the delivery of care and poison the atmosphere of workers' compensation medicine for employers, workers, and medical providers alike. As a specific issue for medical management, the same technologies that today provide better data for treatment planning, utilization review, and record keeping can also be leveraged to perpetuate wholesale fraud. (North, 2010, p. 163)

The system has a bad reputation and is seen as either harmful to workers or rife with fraud.

The general public hears only two stories—workers trying to game the system or workers who fell through the cracks. (IAIABC, 2016a, p. 3)

Performance Measurement

Workers' compensation generates a lot of data but there continues to be a lack of performance measurement and benchmarking in and across jurisdictions. The number of workers' compensation claims filed in a year across the United States is unknown, many jurisdictions do not have a return to work program nor do they track return to work rates, and the reporting of dispute metrics varies and is sometimes nonexistent. For the system to convincingly support its claims of effectiveness, it must focus more on performance measurement. (IAIABC, 2016a, p. 2)

Evidence commonly exists on the costs to employers—and a number of different measures are commonly used. However, evidence about worker outcomes has been much more difficult for policymakers to obtain. Over the past 25 years the availability of tools and metrics of worker outcomes has increased significantly . . . development and testing of a patient satisfaction survey in California; measurement of the effect of treatment guidelines on medical costs and outcomes in Colorado; identification of indicators of the effect of managed care plans on quality of care in Florida; the development of data collection efforts to evaluate managed care programs on costs, quality, and satisfaction in Georgia, New Hampshire, and New York; and a project on quality of care outcomes comparing managed care to traditional fee for service in Washington. (Belton, 2010, p. 101)

Lack of Transparency

Workers' compensation benefits need to be delivered through a transparent process. (IAIABC, 2016b, p. 3)

Lack of Communication Between Stakeholders

The industry must raise awareness about the vital role workers' compensation plays in supporting economic growth. (IAIABC, 2016a, p. 1)

There were many who felt that the grand bargain was an "illusion" and that there is no single bargain. In many ways the grand bargain is really more about the "spirit" of employers and employees coming together and striking an agreeable deal and a concrete quid pro quo. (IAIABC, 2016c, p. 2)

Recognition that injuries and illnesses likely not considered at the beginning of workers' compensation have altered the grand bargain in favor of the employee. (IAIABC, 2016d, p. 2)

References

Asfaw, Abay, Regina Pana-Cryan, Tim Bushnell, and Steven Sauter, "Musculoskeletal Disorders and Associated Healthcare Costs Among Family Members of Injured Workers," *American Journal of Industrial Medicine*, Vol. 58, No. 11, 2015, pp. 1205–1216. As of July 29, 2018: https://onlinelibrary.wiley.com/doi/pdf/10.1002/ajim.22500

Autor, David, and Mark Duggan, "Supporting Work: A Proposal for Modernizing the U.S. Disability Insurance System," The Brookings Institution website, December 3, 2010. As of July 26, 2018: https://www.brookings.edu/research/supporting-work-a-proposal-for-modernizing-the-u-s-disability-insurance-system/

Baicker, Katherine, Sendhil Mullainathan, and Joshua Schwartzstein, "Behavioral Hazard in Health Insurance," *Quarterly Journal of Economics*, Vol. 130, No. 4, 2015, pp. 1623–1667. doi:10.1093/qje/qjv029.

Banerjee, Abhijit V., and Esther Duflo, "The Experimental Approach to Development Economics," *Annual Review of Economics*, Vol. 1, No. 1, 2009, pp. 151–178. doi:10.1146/annurev.economics.050708.143235.

Barth, Peter, "Workers' Compensation Before and After 1983," in R. A. Victor and L. L. Carrubba, eds., *Workers' Compensation: Where Have We Come? Where Are We Going?* Cambridge, Mass.: Workers' Compensation Research Institute, 2010, pp. 3–19.

Belton, Sharon, "Worker Outcomes: Recovery of Health, Access, and Satisfaction with Care," in R. A. Victor and L. L. Carrubba, eds., *Workers' Compensation: Where Have We Come? Where Are We Going?* Cambridge, Mass.: Workers' Compensation Research Institute, 2010, pp. 99–116.

Ben-Shalom, Yonatan, Steve Bruns, Kara Contreary, and David Stapleton, "Stay-at-Work/Return-to-Work: Key Facts, Critical Information Gaps, and Current Practices and Proposals," Washington, D.C.: Mathematica Policy Research, 2017.

Bernhardt, Annette, Ruth Milkman, Nik Theodore, Douglas Heckathorn, Mirabai Auer, James DeFilippis, Ana Luz Gonzalez, et al., "Broken Laws, Unprotected Workers: Violations of Employment and Labor Laws in America's Cities," National Employment Law Project, 2009. As of August 21, 2018: https://www.nelp.org/wp-content/uploads/2015/03/BrokenLawsReport2009.pdf

Bhattacharya, Anasua, and Robert M. Park, "Excess Healthcare Costs Associated with Prior Workers' Compensation Activity," *American Journal of Industrial Medicine*, Vol. 55, No. 11, 2012, pp. 1018–1027. As of July 29, 2018: https://onlinelibrary.wiley.com/doi/pdf/10.1002/ajim.22112

BLS, "Frequently Asked Questions About Data on Contingent and Alternative Employment Arrangements," 2018. As of June 20, 2018:
https://www.bls.gov/cps/contingent-and-alternative-arrangements-faqs.htm

Boden, Leslie I., and Monica Galizzi, "Blinded by Moral Hazard," *Rutgers University Law Review*, Vol. 69, 2016, pp. 1213–1232. As of July 28, 2018:
https://heinonline.org/HOL/Page?collection=journals&handle=hein.journals/rutlr69&id=1245

Boden, Leslie I., and Emily A. Spieler, "The Relationship Between Workplace Injuries and Workers' Compensation Claims: The Importance of System Design," in R. A. Victor and L. L. Carrubba, eds., *Workers' Compensation: Where Have We Come? Where Are We Going?* Cambridge, Mass.: Workers' Compensation Research Institute, 2010, pp. 215–234.

Bruns, Daniel, Kathryn Mueller, and Pamela A. Warren, "Biopsychosocial Law, Health Care Reform, and the Control of Medical Inflation in Colorado," *Rehabilitation Psychology*, Vol. 57, No. 2, 2012, p. 81.

Burton, John F., "Comments: 'Workers' Compensation at a Crossroads: Back to the Future or Back to the Drawing Board?'" in Pound Institute/Rutgers/Northeastern Symposium, *The Demise of the Grand Bargain: Compensation for Injured Workers in the 21st Century*, 2016. As of July 26, 2018:
http://poundinstitute.org/content/2016-symposium-papers

———, "National Developments in Workers' Compensation: Nullifying the Grand Bargain?" *Workers' First Watch*, Winter 2017, Workers' Injury Law and Advocacy Group, No. 1, 2017, pp. 53–66.

Carre, Francoise, "(In) Dependent Contractor Misclassification," Economic Policy Institute Briefing Paper, 2015. As of August 17, 2018:
https://www.epi.org/publication/independent-contractor-misclassification/

Chari, Ramya, Chia-Chia Chang, Steven L. Sauter, Elizabeth L. Petrun Sayers, Jennifer L. Cerully, Paul Schulte, Anita L. Schill, and Lori Uscher-Pines, "Expanding the Paradigm of Occupational Safety and Health: A New Framework for Worker Well-Being," *Journal of Occupational and Environmental Medicine*, Vol. 60, No. 7, 2018, pp. 589–593.

Chernew, Michael E., Allison B. Rosen, and A. Mark Fendrick, "Value-Based Insurance Design," *Health Affairs*, Vol. 2, No. 2, 2010, pp. 1–16. doi:10.1377/hlthaff.26.2.w195.

Chetty, Raj, and Amy Finkelstein, "Social Insurance: Connecting Theory to Data," *Handbook of Public Economics*, Vol. 5, 2013, pp. 111–193. doi:10.1016/B978-0-444-53759-1.00003-0.

CMS, "Workers' Compensation Medicare Set-Aside Arrangement (WCMSA) Reference Guide," 2018. As of July 26, 2018:
https://www.cms.gov/Medicare/Coordination-of-Benefits-and-Recovery/Workers-Compensation-Medicare-Set-Aside-Arrangements/WCMSA-Overview.html

Commonwealth of Massachusetts, "Temporary Workers," webpage, mass.gov, undated. As of August 6, 2018:
https://www.mass.gov/service-details/temporary-workers

Crum, Elizabeth, "Workers' Compensation Adjudication and Administration," in R. A. Victor and L. L. Carrubba, eds., *Workers' Compensation: Where Have We Come? Where Are We Going?* Cambridge, Mass.: Workers' Compensation Research Institute, 2010, pp. 185–196.

Davoli, Charles, "Challenges of the Changing Legal Structure of Workers' Compensation and the Changing Workforce," in Pound Institute/Rutgers/Northeastern Symposium, *The Demise of the Grand Bargain: Compensation for Injured Workers in the 21st Century*, 2016. As of July 26, 2018:
http://poundinstitute.org/content/2016-symposium-papers

Deaton, Angus, "Instruments, Randomization, and Learning About Development," *Journal of Economic Literature*, Vol. 48, No. 2, 2010, pp. 424–455. doi:10.1257/jel.48.2.424.

DOL, "Does the Workers' Compensation System Fulfill Its Obligations to Injured Workers?" 2016. As of July 28, 2018:
https://www.dol.gov/asp/WorkersCompensationSystem/WorkersCompensationSystemReport.pdf

DOL ODEP, "S@W/R2W Research & RETAIN Demonstration Projects," 2018. As of May 25, 2018:
https://www.dol.gov/odep/topics/SAW-RTW/news-events.htm

Duff, Michael, "More Contractual Opt-Out: The Gig Race to the Bottom Rolls on to Georgia and Back to the 19th Century," *Workers' Compensation Law Prof Blog*, March 27, 2018. As of July 26, 2018:
http://lawprofessors.typepad.com/workerscomplaw/2018/03/more-contractual-opt-out-the-gig-race-to-the-bottom-rolls-on-to-georgia-and-back-to-the-19th-century.html

Fishback, Price V., and Shawn E. Kantor, *A Prelude to the Welfare State: The Origins of Workers' Compensation*. Chicago, Ill.: University of Chicago Press, 2007.

Foley, Michael, "Factors Underlying Observed Injury Rate Differences Between Temporary Workers and Permanent Peers," *American Journal of Industrial Medicine*, Vol. 60, No. 10, 2017, pp. 841–851. doi:10.1002/ajim.22763.

Fomenko, Olesya, and Te-Chun Liu, "Designing Workers' Compensation Fee Schedules, 2016," Workers Compensation Research Institute website, 2016. As of July 26, 2018:
https://www.wcrinet.org/reports/designing-workers-compensation-medical-fee-schedules-2016

Forst, Linda, Lee Friedman, and Abraham Chukwu, "Reliability of the AMA Guides to the Evaluation of Permanent Impairment," *Journal of Occupational and Environmental Medicine*, Vol. 52, No. 12, 2010, pp. 1201–1203.

Franklin, Gary M., Ã. Jaymie Mai, Thomas Wickizer, Judith A. Turner, Deborah Fulton-Kehoe, and Linda Grant, "Opioid Dosing Trends and Mortality in Washington State Workers' Compensation, 1996–2002," *American Journal of Industrial Medicine*, Vol. 49, May 2005, pp. 91–99. doi:10.1002/ajim.20191.

Franklin, Gary M., Thomas M. Wickizer, Norma B. Coe, and Deborah Fulton-Kehoe, "Workers' Compensation: Poor Quality Health Care and the Growing Disability Problem in the United States," *American Journal of Industrial Medicine*, Vol. 58, No. 3, 2015, pp. 245–251. doi:10.1002/ajim.22399.

Galizzi, Monica, Roberto Leombruni, Lia Pacelli, and Antonella Bena, "Injured Workers and Their Return to Work: Beyond Individual Disability and Economic Incentives," *Evidence-Based IIRM: A Global Forum for Empirical Scholarship*, Vol. 4, No. 1, 2016, pp. 2–29.

Gaynor, Martin, and Robert Town, "The Impact of Hospital Consolidation—Update," *Robert Wood Johnson Foundation Policy Brief*, Vol. 9, June 2012, pp. 1–8. doi:10.13140/RG.2.1.4294.0882.

Grabell, Michael, and Howard Berkes, "How Much Is Your Arm Worth? Depends on Where You Work," *ProPublica*, March 5, 2015a. As of July 26, 2018:
https://www.propublica.org/article/how-much-is-your-arm-worth-depends-where-you-work
——— , "The Demolition of Workers' Comp," *ProPublica*, March 4, 2015b. As of July 26, 2018:
https://www.propublica.org/article/the-demolition-of-workers-compensation
——— , "Inside Corporate America's Campaign to Ditch Workers' Comp," *ProPublica*, October 14, 2015c. As of July 26, 2018:
https://www.propublica.org/article/inside-corporate-americas-plan-to-ditch-workers-comp

Groeger, Lena, Michael Grabell, and Cynthia Cotts, "Workers' Comp Benefits: How Much Is a Limb Worth?" *ProPublica*, March 5, 2015. As of July 26, 2018:
https://projects.propublica.org/graphics/workers-compensation-benefits-by-limb

Grossman, Michael, "On the Concept of Health Capital and the Demand for Health," *Journal of Political Economy*, Vol. 80, No. 2, 1972, pp. 223–255.

Horejsh, Jennifer Wolf, "Workers' Compensation SWOT Analysis," *Accidentally* (podcast), 2017. As of July 26, 2018:
https://www.iaiabc.org/iaiabc/Accidentally_Podcasts.asp; (episodes parts 1 and 2)
https://soundcloud.com/iaiabc/workers-compensation-swot-part-1 and
https://soundcloud.com/iaiabc/workers-compensation-swot-part-2

Hunt, H. Allan, "Wage Replacement Benefits," in R. A. Victor and L. L. Carrubba, eds., *Workers' Compensation: Where Have We Come? Where Are We Going?* Cambridge, Mass.: Workers' Compensation Research Institute, 2010, pp. 79–98.

Hunt, H. Allan, and Peter S. Barth, "Compromise and Release Settlements in Workers' Compensation: Final Report," report prepared for Washington L&I, 2010. As of August 17, 2018: http://research.upjohn.org/cgi/viewcontent.cgi?article=1181&context=reports

Hunt, H. Allan, and Marcus Dillender, *Workers' Compensation: Analysis for Its Second Century*. Kalamazoo, Mich.: W. E. Upjohn Institute for Employment Research, 2017.

Hyatt, Henry, "The Closure Effect: Evidence from Workers' Compensation Litigation," U.S. Census Bureau Center for Economic Studies Paper No. CES-WP-10-01, January 1, 2010. doi:10.2139/ssrn.1531603.

IAIABC, "Final Report," in IAIABC National Conversations on the Future of Workers' Compensation, *National Conversations*, 2016a. As of July 26, 2018: https://www.iaiabc.org/iaiabc/National_Conversations1.asp

———, "Maine Report," in IAIABC National Conversations on the Future of Workers' Compensation, *National Conversations*, 2016b. As of July 26, 2018: https://www.iaiabc.org/iaiabc/National_Conversations1.asp

———, "New Mexico Report," in IAIABC National Conversations on the Future of Workers' Compensation, *National Conversations*, 2016c. As of July 26, 2018: https://www.iaiabc.org/iaiabc/National_Conversations1.asp

———, "Wisconsin Report," in IAIABC National Conversations on the Future of Workers' Compensation, *National Conversations*, 2016d. As of July 26, 2018: https://www.iaiabc.org/iaiabc/National_Conversations1.asp

IAIABC Disability Management and Return to Work Committee, "Return to Work: A Foundational Approach to Return to Function," 2016. As of July 26, 2018: https://www.iaiabc.org/iaiabc/Disability_Management_and_Return_to_Work_Committee.asp

Illinois General Assembly, "Employment: Day and Temporary Labor Services Act," webpage, ilga.gov, undated. As of August 6, 2018: http://www.ilga.gov/legislation/ilcs/ilcs3.asp?ActID=2417&ChapterID=68

Institute for Health Metrics and Evaluation, "Global Burden of Disease Study, 2016." As of July 26, 2018: https://vizhub.healthdata.org/gbd-compare/#

Kuper, Hannah, and Michael Marmot, "Job Strain, Job Demands, Decision Latitude, and Risk of Coronary Heart Disease Within the Whitehall II Study," *Journal of Epidemiology and Community Health*, Vol. 57, No. 2, 2003, pp. 147–153.

Leigh, J. Paul, and James P. Marcin, "Workers' Compensation Benefits and Shifting Costs for Occupational Injury and Illness," *Journal of Occupational and Environmental Medicine*, Vol. 54, No. 4, 2012, pp. 445–450. doi:10.1097/JOM.0b013e3182451e54.

Levine, David I., Frank Neuhauser, and Jeffrey S. Petersen, "'Carve-Outs' from the Workers' Compensation System," *Journal of Policy Analysis and Management*, Vol. 21, No. 3, 2002, pp. 467–483. As of July 28, 2018: https://onlinelibrary.wiley.com/doi/abs/10.1002/pam.10055

Lipton, Barry, and Karen Ayres, "Workers' Compensation Cost Drivers Through the Years," in R. A. Victor and L. L. Carrubba, eds., *Workers' Compensation: Where Have We Come? Where Are We Going?* Cambridge, Mass.: Workers' Compensation Research Institute, 2010, pp. 21–38.

Lynch, James, "Comments: 'Workers' Compensation at a Crossroads: Back to the Future or Back to the Drawing Board?'" in Pound Institute/Rutgers/Northeastern Symposium, *The Demise of the Grand Bargain: Compensation for Injured Workers in the 21st Century*, 2016. As of July 26, 2018:
http://poundinstitute.org/content/2016-symposium-papers

———, "Economic Incentives in Workers' Compensation: A Holistic, International Perspective," *Rutgers University Law Review*, Vol. 69, 2017, p. 1249. As of July 28, 2018:
https://heinonline.org/HOL/Page?handle=hein.journals/rutlr69&div=37&g_sent=1&casa_tok en=&collection=journals

Malooly, Robert J., "Workers' Compensation Insurance Markets and the Role of State Funds," in R. A. Victor and L. L. Carrubba, eds., *Workers' Compensation: Where Have We Come? Where Are We Going?* Cambridge, Mass.: Workers' Compensation Research Institute, 2010, pp. 39–57.

Marmot, Michael G., Stephen Stansfeld, Chandra Patel, Fiona North, Jenny Head, Ian White, Eric Brunner, Amanda Feeney, and G. Davey Smith, "Health Inequalities Among British Civil Servants: The Whitehall II Study," *The Lancet*, Vol. 337, No. 8754, 1991, pp. 1387–1393.

McLaren, Christopher F., and Marjorie L. Baldwin, "Workers' Compensation: Benefits, Coverage, and Costs (2014 data)," National Academy of Social Insurance (NASI) website, 2016. As of August 17, 2018:
https://www.nasi.org/sites/default/files/research/NASI_Workers_Comp_Report_2016.pdf

McLaren, Christopher F., and Marjorie L. Baldwin, "Workers' Compensation: Benefits, Coverage, and Costs (2015 data)," National Academy of Social Insurance (NASI) website, 2017. As of July 26, 2018:
https://www.nasi.org/sites/default/files/research/NASI_Workers%20Comp%20Report%20 2017_web.pdf

Morantz, Alison, "Workers' Compensation at a Crossroads: Back to the Future or Back to the Drawing Board ?" in Pound Institute/Rutgers/Northeastern Symposium, *The Demise of the Grand Bargain: Compensation for Injured Workers in the 21st Century*, 2016. As of July 26, 2018: http://poundinstitute.org/content/2016-symposium-papers

Morantz, Alison, Julia Bodson, Sarah Michael Levine, and Marcus Vilhelm Palsson, "Economic Incentives in Workers' Compensation: A Holistic, International Perspective," *Rutgers University Law Review*, Vol. 69, 2016, pp. 1015–1080. As of July 28, 2018:
https://heinonline.org/HOL/Page?handle=hein.journals/rutlr69&div=29&g_sent=1&casa_tok en=&collection=journals

Moss, Robert, David McFarland, C. J. Mohin, and Ben Haynes, "Impact on Impairment Ratings from Switching to the American Medical Association's Sixth Edition of the 'Guides to the Evaluation of Permanent Impairment,'" National Council on Compensation Insurance (NCCI) website, 2012. As of July 28, 2018:
https://www.ncci.com/Articles/Documents/II_Impact_of_AMA_Guides.pdf

Mueller, Kathryn L., and Jeffrey S. Harris, "Medical Care in the Next Decade: What the Last 10 Years Have Taught Us," in R. A. Victor and L. L. Carrubba, eds., *Workers' Compensation: Where Have We Come? Where Are We Going?* Cambridge, Mass.: Workers' Compensation Research Institute, 2010, pp. 133–160.

Mueller, Kathryn, Doris Konicki, Paul Larson, T. Warner Hudson, Charles Yarborough, and Marianne Dreger, "Advancing Value-Based Medicine: Why Integrating Functional Outcomes with Clinical Measures Is Critical to Our Health Care Future," *Journal of Occupational and Environmental Medicine*, Vol. 59, No. 4, 2017, pp. e57–62. doi:10.1097/JOM.0000000000001014.

National Commission on State Workmen's Compensation Laws, "The Report of the National Commission on State Workmen's Compensation Laws," Washington, D.C.: SSA, 1972. As of July 27, 2018:
https://www.ssa.gov/policy/docs/ssb/v35n10/v35n10p31.pdf

Neuhauser, Frank, "The Myth of Workplace Injuries," *Perspectives* (IAIABC), April 2016, pp. 16–21.

New York State Occupational Health Clinics Oversight Committee, "Report to the Governor and Legislature," 2012. As of July 27, 2018:
https://www.health.ny.gov/environmental/workplace/occupational_health_clinic/oversight_committee_report.htm

North, David, "Workers' Compensation Medical Management, 1983 to 2008: Innovation, Regulatory Response, and Unfinished Business," in R. A. Victor and L. L. Carrubba, eds., *Workers' Compensation: Where Have We Come? Where Are We Going?* Cambridge, Mass.: Workers' Compensation Research Institute, 2010, pp. 161–184.

NYS OHCN, "New York State Occupational Health Clinic Network Report—Key Updates 2006–2015," 2017. As of July 27, 2018:
https://www.health.ny.gov/environmental/workplace/clinic_network.htm

O'Leary, Paul, Leslie I. Boden, Seth A. Seabury, Al Ozonoff, and Ethan Scherer, "Workplace Injuries and the Take-Up of Social Security Disability Benefits," *Social Security Bulletin*, Vol. 72, No. 3, 2012, pp. 1–17.

Ohio BWC, "Fiscal Year 2017 Report," 2017. As of July 27, 2018:
https://www.bwc.ohio.gov/downloads/blankpdf/AnnualReport.pdf

Oregon DCBS Workers' Compensation Division, "Employer-at-Injury Program (EAIP)," 2018a. As of May 25, 2018:
http://wcd.oregon.gov/rtw/Pages/eaip.aspx

———, "Oregon Preferred Worker Program Fact Sheet," 2018b. As of May 25, 2018:
http://wcd.oregon.gov/Publications/3077.pdf

———, "Preferred Worker Program (PWP)," 2018c. As of May 25, 2018:
http://wcd.oregon.gov/rtw/Pages/pwp.aspx

———, "The Employer-at-Injury Program," 2018d. As of May 25, 2018:
http://wcd.oregon.gov/Publications/3525.pdf

OSHA, "Employer Safety Incentive and Disincentive Policies and Practices," 2012. As of June 18, 2018:

https://www.osha.gov/as/opa/whistleblowermemo.html

OSHA, "Adding Inequality to Injury: The Costs of Failing to Protect Workers on the Job," *Quick Takes*, Vol. 14, No. 6, 2015. As of July 27, 2018:

https://www.osha.gov/as/opa/quicktakes/qt031615.html

Pinnacol Assurance, "Functional Gains and the QPOP Program," 2018. As of July 2, 2018:
https://www.pinnacol.com/sites/default/files/2017-10/Functional-Gains-QPOP-Program
-101017.pdf

Ravesteijn, Bastian, Hans Van Kippersluis, and Eddy Van Doorslaer, "The Wear and Tear on Health: What Is the Role of Occupation?" *Health Economics (United Kingdom)*, Vol. 27, No. 2, 2018, pp. e69–86.
doi:10.1002/hec.3563.

Reville, Robert T., Seth A. Seabury, Frank W. Neuhauser, John F. Burton, Jr., and Michael D. Greenberg, *An Evaluation of California's Permanent Disability Rating System*. Santa Monica, Calif.: RAND Corporation, MG-258-ICJ, 2005. As of July 26, 2018:
https://www.rand.org/pubs/monographs/MG258.html

Robinson, J. C., "Theory and Practice in the Design of Physician Payment Incentives," *The Milbank Quarterly*, Vol. 79, No. 2, 2001, pp. 149–177.
doi:10.1111/1468-0009.00202.

Savych, Bogdan, and H. Allan Hunt, "Adequacy of Workers' Compensation Income Benefits in Michigan," Cambridge, Mass.: Workers Compensation Research Institute, WC-17-20, 2017. As of July 27, 2018:

https://www.wcrinet.org/reports/adequacy-of-workers-compensation-income-benefits-in-
michigan

Savych, Bogdan, and Vennela Thumula, "Comparing Outcomes for Injured Workers in Indiana, 2016 Interviews," Cambridge, Mass.: Workers Compensation Research Institute, 2017. As of July 27, 2018:

https://www.wcrinet.org/reports/comparing-outcomes-for-injured-workers-in-Indiana-2016
-interviews

Seabury, Seth A., Frank Neuhauser, and Teryl Nuckols, "American Medical Association Impairment Ratings and Earnings Losses Due to Disability," *Journal of Occupational and Environmental Medicine*, Vol. 55, No. 3, 2013, pp. 286–291.

Silverstein, Michael, "Preventing Workplace Injuries and Illnesses," in R. A. Victor and L. L. Carrubba, eds., *Workers' Compensation: Where Have We Come? Where Are We Going?* Cambridge, Mass.: Workers' Compensation Research Institute, 2010, pp. 235–250.

Spieler, Emily A., "(Re)Assessing the Grand Bargain: Compensation for Work Injuries in the U.S., 1900–2016," in Pound Institute/Rutgers/Northeastern Symposium, *The Demise of the Grand Bargain: Compensation for Injured Workers in the 21st Century*, 2016. As of July 26, 2018:

http://poundinstitute.org/content/2016-symposium-papers

———, "(Re) Assessing the Grand Bargain: Compensation for Work Injuries in the United States, 1900–2017," *Rutgers University Law Review*, Vol. 69, 2017, pp. 891–1014. As of July 28, 2018:

https://heinonline.org/HOL/Page?handle=hein.journals/rutlr69&div=28&g_sent=1&casa_token=&collection=journals.

Spieler, Emily A., and John F. Burton, "The Lack of Correspondence Between Work-Related Disability and Receipt of Workers' Compensation Benefits," *American Journal of Industrial Medicine*, Vol. 55, No. 6, 2012, pp. 487–505. doi:10.1002/ajim.21034.

Stapleton, David, and Jennifer Christian, "Helping Workers Who Develop Medical Problems Stay Employed: Expanding Washington's COHE Program Beyond Workers' Compensation," Washington, D.C.: Mathematica Policy Research, 2016. As of July 27, 2018:

https://www.mathematica-mpr.com/our-publications-and-findings/publications/helpingworkers-who-develop-medical-problems-stay-employed-expanding-washingtons-coheprogram-beyond.

Steggert, Robert B., "Cost Trends and Cost Drivers: An Employer's Perspective," in R. A. Victor and L. L. Carrubba, eds., *Workers' Compensation: Where Have We Come? Where Are We Going?* Cambridge, Mass.: Workers' Compensation Research Institute, 2010, pp. 59–78.

Strunin, Lee, and Leslie I. Boden, "Family Consequences of Chronic Back Pain," *Social Science and Medicine*, Vol. 58, No. 7, 2004a, pp. 1385–1393.

———, "The Workers' Compensation System: Worker Friend or Foe?" *American Journal of Industrial Medicine*, Vol. 45, No. 4, 2004b, pp. 338–345. http://doi.wiley.com/10.1002/ajim.10356.

Swedlow, Alex, "Social Policies of Disability Evaluation," in R. A. Victor and L. L. Carrubba, eds., *Workers' Compensation: Where Have We Come? Where Are We Going?* Cambridge, Mass.: Workers' Compensation Research Institute, 2010, pp. 197–214.

Szymendera, Scott D., "Workers' Compensation: Overview and Issues," CRS Report R44580, Washington, D.C.: Congressional Research Service, 2017. As of July 27, 2018:

https://digitalcommons.ilr.cornell.edu/key_workplace/1974/

Tanenbaum, Jeffrey, and Alicia Anderson, "California Says Think Twice Before Using Temporary Workers or Others from Staffing Agencies and Other Labor Contractors," January 27, 2015. As of August 6, 2018: https://www.nixonpeabody.com/en/ideas/articles/2015/01/27/california-says-think-twice -before-using-temporary-workers-or-others-from-staffing-agen

Theorell, Töres, Anne Hammarström, Gunnar Aronsson, Lil Träskman Bendz, Tom Grape, Christer Hogstedt, Ina Marteinsdottir, Ingmar Skoog, and Charlotte Hall, "A Systematic Review Including Meta-Analysis of Work Environment and Depressive Symptoms," *BMC Public Health*, Vol. 15, No. 1, 2015, pp. 1–14. doi:10.1186/s12889-015-1954-4.

U.S. Government Accountability Office, 2018, "Social Security Disability Insurance: Information on Potential Implications of Expanding Private Disability Insurance," Washington, D.C.: U.S. Government Accountability Office, gao-18-248, April 10, 2018. As of July 27, 2018: https://www.gao.gov/products/GAO-18-248

Utterback, David F., Alysha R. Meyers, and Steven J. Wurzelbacher, "Workers' Compensation Insurance: A Primer for Public Health." Washington, D.C.: NIOSH, 2014. As of July 27, 2018: https://www.cdc.gov/niosh/docs/2014-110/default.html

Victor, Rick, "Changes to Workers Comp Coverage in the Political Climate," *Workers Comp Matters* (podcast), Legal Talk Network, 2018. As of July 27, 2018: https://legaltalknetwork.com/podcasts/workers-comp-matters/2018/04/changes-to-workers- comp-coverage-in-the-political-climate/

Webb, Mark, Alex Swedlow, and Rena David, "Revisiting 24-Hour Health Care Coverage and Its Integration with the California Workers' Compensation System," *Spotlight Report* (California Workers' Compensation Institute), March 2016.

Wickizer, Thomas M., Gary Franklin, Deborah Fulton-Kehoe, Jeremy Gluck, Robert Mootz, Terri Smith-Weller, and Roy Plaeger-Brockway, "Improving Quality, Preventing Disability and Reducing Costs in Workers' Compensation Healthcare: A Population-Based Intervention Study," *Medical Care*, Vol. 49, No. 12, 2011, pp. 1105–1111.

WorkSafeBC, "The Certificate of Recognition Program—Standards and Guidelines," January 2011, p. 126. As of July 27, 2018: https://www.worksafebc.com/en/resources/health-safety/books-guides/certificate -recognition-cor-standards-guidelines?lang=en

Wurzelbacher, Steven J., "Improving Safety and Health Through Workers' Compensation Systems," *Perspectives* (IAIABC), July 2017, pp. 6–10.

Wurzelbacher, Steven J., Stephen J. Bertke, Michael P. Lampl, P. Timothy Bushnell, Alysha R. Meyers, David C. Robins, and Ibraheem S. Al-Tarawneh, "The Effectiveness of Insurer-Supported Safety and Health Engineering Controls in Reducing Workers' Compensation Claims and Costs," *American Journal of Industrial Medicine*, Vol. 57, 2014, pp. 1398–1412. As of August 17, 2018:
https://www.ncbi.nlm.nih.gov/pmc/articles/PMC4504420

Zaidman, Brian, "Examining the Injuries of Temporary Help Agency Workers," St. Paul, Minn.: Minnesota Department of Labor and Industry, 2017. As of July 27, 2018:
https://static1.squarespace.com/static/55ddc72fe4b0f656b822f51d/t/5a301d5053450af01ffd9a8d/1513102673640/Brian+Zaidman__Ocuupational+Injury_Temp+workers+MIPA+Nov+2017.pdf